D0819675

designer preserves

Patricia Lousada

MARTIN BOOKS

Notes on recipes

All recipes in this book give ingredients in both metric and imperial measures. Use either set of quantities, but not both, in any one recipe. Egg size is medium (size 3) unless otherwise stated.

Published by Martin Books
Simon & Schuster International Group
Fitzwilliam House
32 Trumpington Street
Cambridge CB2 1QY
in association with Tate + Lyle Sugars
Enterprise House
45 Homesdale Road
Bromley
Kent BR2 9TE

First published 1989
© Woodhead-Faulkner Ltd 1989

ISBN 0 85941 597 X

Design: by Design, Newmarket
Photography: Nick Carman
Food preparation for photography: Maxine Clark
Stylist: Penny Mishcon
Typesetting: Goodfellow & Egan Phototypesetting, Cambridge
Printed and bound in Italy by Arnoldo Mondadori Editore, Verona

Contents

Introduction

We all have our favourite jam and jelly recipes which we bring out in the summer time when there is an abundance of soft fruits and berries. Many of us will have another session when the Seville oranges appear after the New Year and when last year's supply of marmalade is getting low.

Preserving does not have to involve long hours of hard work or be confined to these brief periods.

Sugar with Pectin

The good news is that you can now make a jar or two of very special jam in just a few minutes. This is largely due to the recently available product, Sugar with Pectin. Not only does the jam set in a few minutes but, because of the short boiling period, the flavour is wonderful. The longer you have to boil fruit with sugar to obtain a set, the less good the fruit flavour will be. Fruits with a high pectin content have always made good jams because the natural pectin gives a quick set. Now, through the use of this new product, any fruit can be set quickly; the resulting preserve will have an excellent flavour. (There is no need to heat Sugar with Pectin before using it.) Fruit liqueurs can also be used in preserves to give a more concentrated fruit flavour. This book only touches on the possibilities that this new world of preserves contains, encouraging you to invent your own range of special preserves.

Other sugars

Granulated, preserving and lump sugar will all give a clear preserve that needs very little skimming. The advantage of preserving sugar is that the large crystals allow the boiling liquid to circulate freely around the grains. Caster sugar can be used, but needs to be carefully stirred as it can settle on the bottom of the pan. Brown sugars are used in chutneys and some marmalades when the flavour and colour of the sugar is desired.

F r u i t

As well as our own favourite fruits, there is an exotic selection that continually expands to meet our increased interest in foods of all kinds. What better way to capture some of these new tastes than in preserves that can be enjoyed on so many occasions, and make eating a constant source of discovery and pleasure.

Fruit used for jam and jellies should be just ripe. Berries should be dry and in good condition, so pick them on a dry afternoon.

Sometimes fruit has an unnaturally shiny appearance, indicating that a chemical sealant has been sprayed on it. Such fruit should be well washed with soap and hot water and then thoroughly rinsed.

T e s t i n g   t i m e

To test for set, place a teaspoon of jam on an ice-cold saucer and return it to the refrigerator for a few seconds. If a finger is drawn through the jam it should remain separated and not run together. Or test by lifting a wooden spoon over the pan; if the last drops fall slowly back into the pan, rather than running off in a quick stream, the jam is ready; work quickly. If you make jam regularly you will soon be able to tell when it is set by the way it looks when it boils. The longer you boil it, the firmer the set will be.

E q u i p m e n t

Stainless steel and enamel-lined pans (especially heavy-bottomed ones) are safe for all preserves, provided that in all cases the contents come only halfway-up the side once the sugar has been added.

Preserving pans are useful if you make jam regularly and in large batches. Copper or brass preserving pans are attractive and fine for all preserves except those that contain vinegar. The acid reacts with the metal, spoiling both taste and colour, and it may even be harmful.

Aluminium pans are also not recommended for making preserves containing acids, though they can be used if the preserve is boiled up quickly and the acid food does not stay long in contact with the aluminium. The preserve should always be removed from the pan once the setting point has been reached.

A jam funnel or ladle with a pouring lip is a great help for filling jars with the minimum of stickiness. Muslin and jelly bags are used for straining.

Jam jars and lids (with any cardboard lid inserts removed) should be well-washed, then sterilised by boiling or soaking in a mild bleach or Milton solution. If using the latter method, rinse with boiling water to remove any chlorine taste. Dry the jars upside-down in the oven at Gas Mark 3/160°C/ 325°F and fill them while they are still warm.

V a c u u m - s e a l i n g

It is essential to seal the jars effectively to exclude micro-organisms. The most usual way of sealing preserves is by creating a partial vacuum, using Cellophane. Once the preserve is in the jar, cover with a waxed paper disc. The entire surface must be covered by the disc – different sizes are available. Wet the Cellophane on one side and place it, wet-side up, over the jar. The preserve must still be very hot – never warm. Keep the Cellophane in place with a rubber band and then stretch it by gently pulling the edges. The wet Cellophane stretches slightly, then shrinks as it dries, so effecting a vacuum-seal.

You can also use jars with ordinary metal screw-top lids. You can usually buy them in small numbers from bee-equipment suppliers, or you can re-use the ones from commercial jams with new lids. The preserve must be at least 1.5 cm (½ inch) below the top of the jar, and the lid must be screwed shut while the preserve is boiling hot. The air trapped in the jar contracts as it cools and causes a vacuum. Metal lids are not suitable for any preserve containing vinegar.

S t o r i n g

Put preserves in small jars so that they will be used up quickly once they are opened. Store the jars in a cool, dry and dark place. Sugar is a preservative, so if the amount of sugar used is much less than the weight of the fruit in any jam recipe, the preserve should be stored in the refrigerator. Vinegar is also a preservative, so chutneys keep well even with a low sugar content.

When the storage time for a preserve is specified as, for example, vacuum-sealed, 6 months, this is the approximate period for which the preserve will keep; it may well keep perfectly for much longer. Once opened, it is best to transfer the jar or bottle to the fridge.

The preserves for which a refrigeration storage time is specified must be kept in the fridge. Any preserve that is not vacuum-sealed should be stored in the fridge. Any low-sugar preserve or curd that would have a very short shelf-life (even if properly sealed) should be refrigerated.

And the Quangle Wangle said
To himself on the crumpety tree,
'Jam and jelly and bread
are the best of foods for me'
Edward Lear

j e l l i e s

j e l l i e s

L i m e a n d H o n e y J e l l y

300 ml (½ pint) fresh lime juice
2 limes
450 g (1 lb) clear honey
½ bottle of liquid pectin (Certo)

Quantity: 600 ml (1 pint)
Storage: vacuum-sealed, 1 year

First scrub the limes with soap and hot water and rinse very thoroughly. Grate the zest. Strain the lime juice into a heavy-bottomed stainless steel saucepan. Add the zest and honey, and bring to the boil. Pour in the pectin and boil hard for 1 minute. Remove from the heat and stir for another minute.

Then put in warm sterilised jars, cover and seal at once.

R o w a n J e l l y

925 g (2 lb) ripe rowan berries, stripped from their stems
1.3 kg (3 lb) sharp cooking apples
juice of 2 lemons
water
preserving or granulated sugar

Quantity: approx 1.2 litres (2 pints)
Storage: vacuum-sealed, 1 year

Wash and drain the berries and place them in a large saucepan. Wash the apples, removing any blemishes, cut into quarters (with pips and skins), and add them to the pan. Add the lemon juice and enough water barely to cover the fruit. Cover the pan and simmer until the fruit is tender. Tip everything into a scalded jelly bag, and leave to drip overnight. Measure the juice into a pan and to each 600 ml (1 pint) add 450 g (1 lb) of sugar. Heat gently, stirring occasionally, until the sugar is dissolved. Bring to the boil and boil hard for a few minutes. Then test for a set by spooning a little of the mixture onto a saucer, chilling, and seeing if the top wrinkles when you push it with your finger. Put in warm, sterilised jars, cover and seal at once.

THE SUBTLE AND slightly smoky flavour of this jelly makes it an ideal companion for venison or lamb.

Peppered Redcurrant Jelly

1.3 kg (3 lb) redcurrants
600 ml (1 pint) water
300 ml (½ pint) red wine
granulated or preserving
  sugar or Sugar with
  Pectin
2–3 tablespoons black
  peppercorns

Quantity: approx 1.2 litres
  (2 pints)
Storage: vacuum-sealed,
  1 year

Wash the redcurrants carefully, leaving the stalks on. Place the fruit in a non-aluminium pan with the water and wine and simmer, covered, for about 45 minutes or until the currants are very soft. Strain through a scalded jelly bag and leave to drip for several hours. Measure the juice and return it to the pan. Add 450 g (1 lb) of sugar for every 600 ml (1 pint) of juice. Stir over a low heat to dissolve the sugar and then bring to the boil. Boil briskly until the setting point is reached – about 3 minutes if using Sugar with Pectin or 10 minutes for granulated or preserving sugar. Remove from the heat and leave until the jam is half-set. Coarsely crush the peppercorns using a mortar and pestle. Add the peppercorns to the jelly, put in sterilised jars, cover, and seal at once.

THE PERFECT COMPANION to all kinds of game or lamb.

S c e n t e d   G e r a n i u m   J e l l y

2.25 kg (5 lb) apples (crab-
apples or cooking apples)
juice of 2 lemons
water
14 geranium leaves
preserving or granulated
sugar

Quantity: approx 1.2 litres
(2 pints)
Storage: vacuum-sealed,
1 year

Wash the apples and remove any blemishes. Cut them into chunks and place in a large saucepan. Barely cover with water. Then cover the pan and simmer until the apples become a soft pulp. Tip into a scalded jelly bag and leave to drip overnight. Measure 450 g (1 lb) of sugar for each pint of apple juice and set aside. Place the apple juice, lemon juice and 10 geranium leaves in a preserving pan and boil for 15 minutes. Meanwhile, warm the sugar in a low oven. Add the warmed sugar to the preserving pan, stirring to dissolve, and boil for 3 minutes. Test for setting by putting a spoonful of jelly on a plate and cooling in the refrigerator. Remove the leaves and discard.

Place a small fresh leaf in the bottom of each sterilised jar, ladle in the jelly, cover and seal at once.

Variations: For mint jelly follow the same method but substitute a bunch of mint, plus a wine glass of vinegar, for the geranium leaves.

For herb jellies follow the same method but use a bunch of herbs, or one specific herb (such as tarragon) instead of the geranium leaves.

ONE OF THE nicest ways of enjoying this fragrant and delicious jelly is with a cream cheese such as mascarpone or petit-suisse. It is also good with cold meats. Never turn down windfalls – they can be the basis for any number of superb jellies.

Blood Orange Jelly;
Peppered Redcurrant Jelly;
Scented Geranium Jelly

B l o o d   O r a n g e   J e l l y

*3 blood oranges, with some
   red in the skins*
400 ml (14 fl oz) water
*400 g (14 oz) Sugar with
   Pectin*

Quantity: 450 ml (¾ pint)
*Storage: vacuum-sealed,
   1 year*

Scrub the oranges with soap and hot water, and then rinse very thoroughly. Halve the oranges and squeeze out the juice. Strain the juice and reserve it. Chop the orange shells coarsely and add them to a saucepan together with the pips and fibres left in the strainer. Add the water and boil gently for 15 minutes. Strain the liquid, and discard the orange pieces. Measure the liquid and add 275 ml (scant ½ pint) to a clean saucepan. Add the red orange juice to the pan and also the Sugar with Pectin. Bring to a simmer, stirring, until the sugar has dissolved. Then boil rapidly for about 2–3 minutes. Pour into sterilised jars, cover, and seal at once.

THE BEAUTIFUL RED colour and fresh taste of this jelly gives it special appeal. Use it for glazing tarts or for spreading on toast.

Raspberry Jelly

1 kg (2¼ lb) raspberries
Sugar with Pectin

Quantity: approx 1.2 litres
(2 pints)
Storage: vacuum-sealed,
1 year

Whizz the fruit in a blender or food processor until puréed. Then pour it into a heavy saucepan. Bring very slowly to the boil and simmer just long enough for the juices to be drawn out, about 5 minutes. Pour into a jelly bag and leave to drip overnight. Measure the juice into a clean pan and allow 450 g (1 lb) of Sugar with Pectin for every 600 ml (1 pint) of juice. Heat the juice, add the sugar, and stir until it is dissolved. Let it come to a rolling boil and boil for about 2–3 minutes. Put in sterilised jars, cover, and seal at once.

Note: By placing a scented geranium leaf in the bottom of the jar before pouring in the raspberry jelly, you will create an intriguing new flavour. The leaf will float to the top as the jar is filled and can be removed once the jelly is opened.

THE SHARP-SCENTED flavour of raspberries makes them ideal for jams and jellies. This jelly is both beautiful to look at and to taste.

Chilli Jelly

3–4 fresh green chillies
2 green peppers, de-seeded
   and chopped roughly
300 ml (½ pint) cider
   vinegar
800 g (1 lb 12 oz)
   granulated sugar
175 ml (6 fl oz) liquid
   pectin (Certo)

Quantity: 600 ml (1 pint)
Storage: vacuum-sealed,
   1 year

Place the chillies, peppers and the vinegar in a food processor, and use the metal blade until the peppers are finely ground. Scrape the mixture into a heavy non-aluminium saucepan. Add the sugar and stir over a medium-high heat until the liquid comes to a full rolling boil. Boil for 10 minutes. Remove from the heat and stir in the pectin. Pour immediately into hot sterilised jars, cover, and seal.

Quince Jelly

2 kg (4 lb 6 oz) quinces
925 g (2 lb) crab-apples or
   other sharp apples
water
1 stick of cinnamon
4 cloves
4 green cardamom pods,
   crushed
granulated sugar

Quantity: approx 1.2 litres
   (2 pints)
Storage: vacuum-sealed,
   1 year

Wash the fruit and scrub the quinces with a brush to remove the down. Rinse thoroughly. Cut away any blemishes from both quinces and apples and discard. Cut the fruit coarsely and place in a pan with the cinnamon stick, cloves and cardamom pods. Cover with water, then cover the pan and simmer until the fruit is tender. Break it up with a potato masher and continue to boil until the fruit is pulpy. Pour into a jelly bag and leave overnight to drip. Measure the juice and allow 450 g (1 lb) of sugar per 600 ml (1 pint). Place the juice and sugar in a preserving pan and bring to a boil, stirring. Boil hard until set lightly when tested. Strain into sterilised jars, cover and seal at once. Store in a cool, dry cupboard.

Looks can be deceiving – it's eating

that's believing

James Thurber

marmalades & mincemeats

Lemon and Lime Marmalade

450 g (1 lb) lemons
450 g (1 lb) limes
1.75 litres (3 pints) water
1.3 kg (3 lb) Sugar with
   Pectin

Quantity: 2 litres
   (3½ pints)
Storage: vacuum-sealed,
   1 year

Scrub the fruit with soap and water, if it has been sealed, and rinse thoroughly. Line a sieve with a round of muslin and place this over a bowl. Cut each fruit in half, squeezing out the juice, pips and pulp, and strain through the lined sieve. Tie up the muslin containing the pips and pulp and place it with the juice into a preserving pan.

Cut the squeezed lemon and lime halves into very fine strips. Add them to the pan, and then cover with the water. Simmer gently for about one hour until the peel is tender. Squeeze all the liquid possible from the bag into the pan and discard the bag. Add the sugar and bring slowly to the boil. Then cook rapidly for about 5 minutes until the marmalade has set. Put in sterilised jars, cover, and seal at once.

K u m q u a t   M a r m a l a d e

450 g (1 lb) kumquats
water
1 lemon
300 g (10 oz) Sugar with
  Pectin

Quantity: 600 ml (1 pint)
Storage: vacuum-sealed,
  1 year

Wash the kumquats and place them in a saucepan, barely covering them with water. Simmer gently for about 10 minutes, or until the skins of the kumquats are tender. Strain, reserving the liquid. When the kumquats have cooled down cut them into thin slices. Reserve the pips. Squeeze the lemons, reserving both the juice and pips. Place the sliced kumquats and lemon juice in a heavy-bottomed saucepan. Tie the pips of both fruit in a muslin bag and add to the pan. Top up the reserved liquid with water to measure 600 ml (1 pint) and add this to the kumquats. Simmer the fruit for 5 minutes before adding the sugar. Bring to the boil and boil for 15–20 minutes until the marmalade has set. Put in sterilised jars, cover, and seal immediately.

Orange Marmalade with Coriander

2 kg (4 lb 6 oz) Seville
  oranges
2 tablespoons coriander
  seeds
water
3 kg (6 lb 9 oz) preserving
  or granulated sugar
150 ml (¼ pint) whisky

Quantity: 2.5 litres
  (4½ pints)
Storage: vacuum-sealed,
  1 year

Scrub the oranges with soap and hot water to remove any dirt and chemicals and rinse thoroughly. Place them in a large saucepan and cover with water. Simmer for about 1½ hours or until the skins of the oranges can be easily pricked with a fork. Strain the oranges, reserving the cooking liquid.

Cut the oranges into thin slivers, reserving all the pips. Place the pips in a muslin bag with the coriander seeds. Measure the cooking liquid and top up with water to make 2.5 litres (4 pints). Place the cooking liquid, oranges, muslin bag and sugar in a large bowl and leave for 24 hours, stirring occasionally to dissolve the sugar. The next day pour the contents of the bowl into a preserving pan and bring to a boil. Boil rapidly until the setting point is reached and it thickens. Remove from the heat and add the whisky. Remove the muslin bag, squeezing out any liquid.

Put in sterilised jars, cover, and seal quickly.

A TRADITIONAL MARMALADE with extra zip.

Kumquat Marmalade
Orange Marmalade with Coriander;
Pineapple Marmalade;

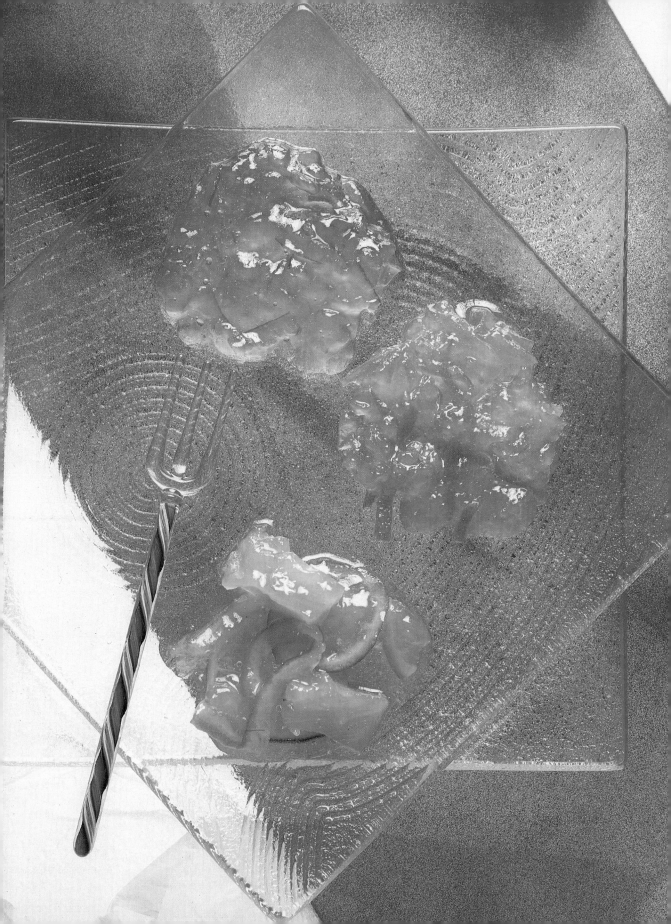

Pineapple Marmalade

*1 medium-sized firm but
ripe pineapple (with a
good pineapple scent)*
*925 g (2 lb) Sugar with
Pectin*
3 limes
2 thin-skinned oranges
900 ml (1½ pints) water

*Quantity: approx 1.2 litres
(2 pints)*
*Storage: vacuum-sealed,
1 year*

Use a serrated knife to cut off both ends of the pineapple, and then slice between the rows of eyes. Remove the hard core and reserve. Peel off the skin and discard. Cut the slices into chunks and place them in a bowl with half the sugar. Wash the limes and oranges with hot water and soap, then rinse thoroughly. Squeeze them then cut them into thin slices. Put all the seeds and the pineapple core in a muslin bag. Put the lime and orange slices in a saucepan with the muslin bag. Add the water and simmer for about 45 minutes, or until the peel is soft. Remove the bag, squeezing out as much liquid as possible. Add the pineapple and remaining sugar. Bring to a boil carefully to dissolve the sugar. Then boil hard for 10–15 minutes until the marmalade has set. Pour into hot sterilised jars, cover, and seal at once.

A TROPICAL-TASTING marmalade with a sweet but refreshing tang.

De Luxe Mincemeat for Vegetarians

300 ml (½ pint) dry cider
225 g (8 oz) dark-brown
  soft sugar
925 g (2 lb) cooking apples,
  peeled, cored and
  chopped
1 teaspoon mixed spice
several gratings of fresh
  nutmeg
½ teaspoon cinnamon
225 g (8 oz) stoned raisins
120 g (4 oz) currants
120 g (4 oz) sultanas
30 g (1 oz) glacé cherries
30 g (1 oz) cut mixed peel
60 g (2 oz) blanched
  almonds
juice and finely grated zest
  of 1 lemon
150 ml (¼ pint) brandy or
  rum

Quantity: 1.2 litres
  (2 pints)
Storage: vacuum-sealed,
  1 year

Heat the cider and sugar together until the sugar dissolves. Then add the chopped apples and spices. Chop the dried fruit and nuts together and add to the pan with the lemon juice and zest. Bring to the boil and simmer gently, uncovered, until the mixture is thick and the apples have become a purée.

Remove from the heat and leave to cool. Stir in the brandy or rum. Put in sterilised jars, cover, and seal at once. Store in a cool, dry place and leave for at least 6 weeks before using.

NON-VEGETARIANS TOO will enjoy mince pies with this scrumptious mixture.

Special Mincemeat with Brandy

120 g (4 oz) raisins
120 g (4 oz) currants
140 g (5 oz) sultanas
30 g (1 oz) glacé cherries
30 g (1 oz) cut mixed peel
120 g (4 oz) cooking apples,
* peeled and cored*
85 g (3 oz) pecans or
* walnuts, chopped*
120 g (4 oz) shredded suet
225 g (8 oz) demerara
* sugar*
1 teaspoon mixed spice
a few gratings of fresh
* nutmeg*
grated zest of 1 lemon
brandy

Quantity: 1.2 litres
* (2 pints)*
Storage: vacuum-sealed,
* 1 year*

Finely chop the fruit peel, apples and nuts and place them in a bowl. Stir in the suet, sugar, spices, lemon zest, and enough brandy to give a moist mixture. Cover and leave for 2 days in a cool place. Stir the mixture and add a bit more brandy. Place into sterilised jars, cover, and seal at once. Allow to mature for at least 4 weeks before using.

MINCE PIES MADE with this very special mincemeat will be a real Christmas treat and could solve a few Christmas presents too. The best candied peel is sold in large pieces; if it is available, double the amount of peel given in the recipe and omit the lemon zest.

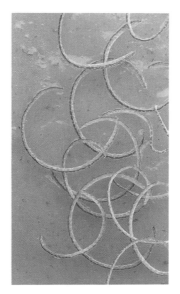

The rule is jam tomorrow and jam
yesterday, but never jam today
Lewis Carroll

Tomato Curd

450 g (1 lb) tomatoes
85 g (3 oz) butter
170 g (6 oz) granulated
   sugar
juice and grated zest of
   1 lemon
2 eggs, well beaten

Quantity: 600 ml (1 pint)
Storage: refrigerated,
   4 weeks

Wash the tomatoes before chopping them. Place the pieces in a small saucepan with a few tablespoons of water. Simmer gently until tender, and then sieve. Place the purée, butter, sugar, lemon juice and zest in a heavy-bottomed, non-aluminium saucepan and cook gently until the sugar dissolves. Add the eggs and continue to cook very gently, stirring with a wooden spoon, until the mixture thickens. Do not allow it to come near the boil. The curd will set thicker as it cools. Put into warm, sterilised jars, cover, and seal at once. Store in the refrigerator and use within 1 month.

Seville Orange Curd

2 large eggs (size 1–2)
2 egg yolks
120 g (4 oz) granulated
   sugar
120 g (4 oz) unsalted
   butter, cut into small
   pieces
zest and juice of 2 Seville
   oranges

Quantity: approx 300 ml
   (½ pint)
Storage: refrigerated,
   4 weeks

Whisk the eggs, egg yolks and sugar together. Pour into a heavy-bottomed, non-aluminium saucepan and add the butter, orange zest and juice. Stir over a very gentle heat (a simmering disc is useful here) until the curd thickens slightly. Do not allow it to come near a simmer. The curd will thicken more as it cools. Pour into a sterilised jar, cover, and seal. Keep refrigerated and use within one month.

ANOTHER EXCELLENT CURD that is wonderful as a spread on toast or as a filling for tarts.

Orange Liqueur Butter

3 oranges
6 sugar cubes
45 g (1½ oz) caster sugar
225 g (8 oz) unsalted butter
*   at room temperature*
3 tablespoons orange
*   liqueur, (such as*
*   Cointreau or Grand*
*   Marnier)*

Quantity: approx 600 ml
*   (1 pint)*
Storage: refrigerated,
*   2 weeks*
*   frozen, 3 months*

Wash two of the oranges with soap and hot water, rinse thoroughly, and dry them. Rub the sugar cubes over the washed oranges until they are impregnated with orange oil, and then place them on a chopping board. Peel off the zest from the 2 oranges with a potato peeler and place on the board with the caster sugar. Chop the zest and sugars very finely. Cream the butter until it is light and fluffy, and then add the orange sugar, mixing until smooth. Squeeze the juice from the 3 oranges and strain – you will need 200 ml (6 fl oz). Beat the orange juice into the butter a few drops at a time. Then add the orange liqueur. Cover and refrigerate or freeze. Re-heat gently if using hot. Bring to room temperature if using as a spread.

THIS IS DELICIOUS heated and poured over hot crêpes. You can also flame the crêpes with a few tablespoons of an orange liqueur to give you crêpes suzettes. The butter can also be used cold as a filling for sponge cakes.

Sara's Cranberry Orange Curd

225 g (8 oz) cranberries
4 tablespoons water
60 g (2 oz) butter
120 g (4 oz) granulated
  sugar
juice of ½ lemon
juice of 1 orange
2 eggs, well beaten

Quantity: 600 ml (1 pint)
Storage: refrigerated,
  4 weeks

Place the cranberries and the water in a small, heavy-bottomed, non-aluminium saucepan. Cover, and cook over a low heat until the fruit has softened. Sieve the fruit into another heavy-bottomed saucepan, and add the butter, sugar, lemon and orange juice. Stir over a low heat until the sugar dissolves then add the well-beaten eggs. Stir with a wooden spoon until the curd thickens. Do not allow it to boil. Pour the curd into hot, sterilised jars, cover, and seal. Store in the refrigerator when cool.

MY AMERICAN NIECE, Sara, helped me with the cooking for this book and invented this curd in the process.

Raspberry Curd

340 g (12 oz) raspberries
120 g (4 oz) cooking apples,
  peeled, cored and
  chopped
juice of 1 large lemon
120 g (4 oz) unsalted butter
340 g (12 oz) granulated
  sugar
4 eggs, beaten

Quantity: approx 900 ml
  (1½ pints)
Storage: refrigerated,
  4 weeks

Place the raspberries and apples in a pan and cook them very slowly until the fruit softens. Then sieve the mixture. Place the fruit, lemon juice, butter and sugar in a heavy-bottomed, non-aluminium saucepan and cook over a gentle heat until the sugar melts. Add the beaten eggs and continue to cook gently, stirring with a wooden spoon, until the mixture thickens. Do not allow it to come near the boil. Put into sterilised jars, cover, and seal at once. Store in the refrigerator and use within one month.

Lime Curd

Sara's Cranberry Orange Curd;

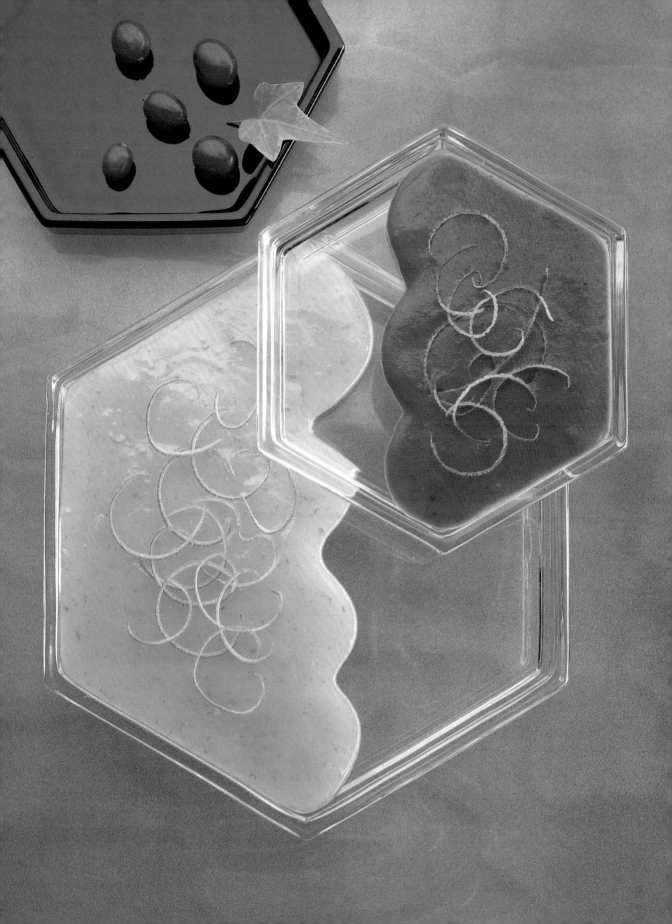

Lime Curd

225 g (8 oz) granulated
   sugar
4 eggs
juice of 4 limes
grated zest of 2 limes
120 g (4 oz) unsalted
   butter, cut into pieces

Quantity: 600 ml (1 pint)
Storage: refrigerated,
   4 weeks

Whisk the sugar and eggs together. Add the lime juice and zest and then the butter. The curd can be cooked over a direct, even heat if you have a very heavy-bottomed, non-aluminium pan and are prepared to stir it religiously. It is safer (but longer) to use a double boiler set over barely simmering water. Although you must keep an eye on it there is no need to stir continuously. Whatever method you use, do not allow the curd to come near to a boil. When it has thickened, pour into hot sterilised jars, cover, and seal at once. Keep refrigerated and use within one month.

Quince Purée with Cardamom

1 large quince
1 tablespoon lime juice
4 green cardamom pods,
   crushed
85 g (3 oz) granulated
   sugar

Quantity: 450 ml (¾ pint)
Storage: refrigerated,
   3 weeks
   frozen, 6 months

Peel, core and cut the quince into chunks. Place these in a saucepan with the lime juice, cardamom and 150 ml (¼ pint) of water. Simmer gently, covered, until the quince is tender. Add the sugar, and when it has dissolved strain through a fine sieve. Adjust the flavour by adding more sugar or lime juice as necessary. Put into hot, sterilised jars, cover, and seal at once.

THERE ARE MANY wonderful ways you can enjoy this intriguing and almost addictive purée. Try it with pork or game or use it to flavour yogurt or cream cheese.

Quince Paste with Pistachio Nuts

juice of 2 lemons
1 kg (2¼ lb) quinces
150 ml (¼ pint) water
1 kg (2¼ lb) granulated
  sugar
120 g (4 oz) shelled
  pistachio nuts, chopped
caster sugar

Quantity: approx 925 g
  (2 lb)
Storage: in an air-tight jar,
  1½ years

Add half the lemon juice to a large bowl of cold water. Peel, core and cut the quinces into slices, dropping them into the acidulated water as they are ready. Drain the quinces and place them in a large heavy-bottomed saucepan with the remaining lemon juice and the water. Cover and cook very gently, stirring occasionally, until the quince is soft. Sieve the quince and return to a clean pan. Add the granulated sugar and cook over a moderate heat, stirring until the mixture is very stiff and jam-like. Remove from the heat and stir in the pistachio nuts. Spread about 1 cm (½ inch) thick in shallow trays lined with greaseproof or bakewell paper. If you cannot get a smooth layer, wait for it to cool down and press it smooth with wet hands.

Place the trays in an airing-cupboard or other dry warm place. When it is dry, cut with a hot knife. Dip in caster sugar (vanilla, if possible) and store in an air-tight container, layered with greaseproof or bakewell paper.

A REAL TREAT to offer guests with after-dinner coffee.

Spiced Prune Butter

450 g (1 lb) prunes
1 tea bag
water
1 navel orange
½ teaspoon each of ground
   cloves and cinnamon
¼ teaspoon ground ginger
juice and grated zest of
   1 lime
70 g (2½ oz) sultanas
300 g (10 oz) granulated
   sugar
60 g (2 oz) shelled pecans,
   chopped

Quantity: 600 ml (1 pint)
Storage: vacuum-sealed,
   6 months
   frozen, 1 year

Place the prunes and tea bag in a bowl. Pour over enough boiling water to cover the fruit and leave for 24 hours. Drain the fruit over a measuring cup and add just enough water to the drained liquid to make 300 ml (½ pint). Pour this into a saucepan along with the fruit. Grate the zest from the orange and add this to the prunes. Cut away all the pith from the orange, thinly slice the flesh, and add it to the prunes. Bring to a boil and simmer for 10 minutes. Add the spices, juice and zest of the lime, sultanas and sugar. Then stir until the sugar has dissolved. Continue to cook for about 8 minutes until the mixture thickens. Then stir in the pecans.

Put in sterilised jars, cover, and seal at once.

Spiced Pear Butter;
Apple Brandy Butter;
Spiced Prune Butter

Apple Brandy Butter

1 kg (2¼ lb) eating apples
300 ml (½ pint) apple juice
3 cloves
5 cm (2-inch) piece of
   cinnamon stick
2 blades of mace
juice and grated zest of
   1 lemon
6 tablespoons orange
   blossom honey
150 ml (¼ pint) Calvados

Quantity: approx 1.2 litres
   (2 pints)
Storage: vacuum-sealed,
   3 months

Wash and then quarter the apples. Place the pieces in a large saucepan with the apple juice, cloves, cinnamon stick and mace. Simmer gently, covered, until the apples turn into a pulp. Sieve the apple purée. Then pour it back into a clean pan and simmer over a gentle heat, stirring continuously to thicken the purée further. Add the lemon juice and zest, honey and Calvados. Continue to cook gently, stirring, until the mixture is very thick. Spoon into jars, cover, and seal immediately.

Spiced Pear Butter

*1 kg (2¼ lb) passacrassana
   or comice pears*
zest and juice of 1 lemon
*170 g (6 oz) granulated
   sugar*
*45 g (1½ oz) light-brown
   sugar*
*5 cm (2-inch) piece of
   cinnamon stick*
*4 green cardamom pods,
   crushed*
3 cloves
*6 tablespoons eau de vie de
   poire William*
*85 g (3 oz) shelled pecans,
   chopped*

Quantity: 600 ml (1 pint)
*Storage: refrigerated,
   3 months
   frozen, 1 year*

Peel, quarter and core the pears. Shred them in a food processor, using the shredding disc, or use the largest holes on a grater. Place the shredded pears in a saucepan with the lemon zest and juice and sugars. Tie the spices in a muslin bag and add to the pan. Stir continuously over a medium heat until the mixture thickens. Add the eau de vie de poire William and cook for a few more minutes. Remove from the heat. Toast the chopped nuts in the oven at Gas Mark 4/180°C/350°F for 6 minutes or until they are lightly toasted. Cool the nuts before stirring them into the pear mixture. Put in jars, cover, and seal at once.

Chocolate Apple Spread

juice and grated zest of
  1 lemon
225 g (8 oz) cooking apples
225 g (8 oz) eating apples
340 g (12 oz) granulated
  sugar
30 g (1 oz) cocoa powder
  (not drinking chocolate)
1–2 teaspoons ground
  cinnamon (optional)

Quantity: 900 ml
  (1½ pints)
Storage: vacuum-sealed,
  6 months
  frozen, 9 months

Place the lemon juice and zest in a saucepan. Peel, core and slice the apples into the pan, turning them in the lemon juice to prevent discolouration. Mix the sugar with the cocoa and add to the pan. Add the cinnamon, if using. Bring slowly to the boil, and continue to simmer slowly, stirring with a wooden spoon. Once the apples have softened, the mixture can be passed through a sieve and returned to the pan if you want a very smooth spread. Continue to simmer the purée, stirring, until the mixture is very thick. Ladle while still boiling hot into warm, sterilised jars, cover, and seal immediately.

Olive Paste

340 g (12 oz) stoned black
  olives
120 g (4 oz) anchovy fillets,
  drained
3 tablespoons capers,
  drained
juice of half a lemon
175 ml (6 fl oz) extra-virgin
  olive oil
freshly ground black pepper

Quantity: 450 ml (¾ pint)
Storage: refrigerated,
  6 months

Place the olives, anchovies and capers in a food processor. Blend to a smooth purée. Scoop the purée out into a bowl and stir in the lemon juice. Stir in the olive oil, a trickle at a time, as if you were making mayonnaise, and add several good grindings of black pepper. Spoon into small sterilised jars, cover, and seal at once.

AN EXCELLENT SPREAD for toast or, mixed with fromage frais, as a stuffing for cherry tomatoes.

Appetite comes with eating
François Rabelais

F r a m b o i s e   J a m

450 g (1 lb) fresh or frozen
raspberries
225 g (8 oz) Sugar with
Pectin
6 tablespoons eau de vie de
framboise

Quantity: 600 ml (1 pint)
Storage: refrigerated,
2 months

Place all the ingredients in a heavy-bottomed saucepan. Bring to the boil over a medium heat. Then boil rapidly for about 5 minutes until set. Pour into sterilised jars, cover, and seal at once.

YOU WILL BE delighted with the results of this raspberry jam and it can be made in the winter months from frozen raspberries. It is very quick to make and a lovely gift for any discerning palate.

C a r a m e l i s e d   A p p l e   J a m

juice and grated zest of
1 lemon
1.2 kg (2½ lb) cooking
apples
450 g (1 lb) granulated
sugar
8 tablespoons water
3 tablespoons brandy

Quantity: approx 1.5 litres
(2½ pints)
Storage: refrigerated,
3 months

Put the lemon juice and zest in a large bowl. Wash, peel, core and dice the apples; add them to the bowl as you go along and toss in the lemon juice.

Place half the sugar in a large heavy-bottomed saucepan and add the water. Bring the sugar to the boil and cook until the sugar caramelises to a golden brown colour. Remove from the heat and add the apples, keeping your face averted, as the hot caramel mixture can spit. Stir the apples and caramel over a medium heat and add the remaining sugar. Return to a boil and cook, stirring all the time, until the mixture is quite thick. Remove from the heat and add the brandy. Spoon into sterilised jars, cover, and seal. Refrigerate when cool.

Peach and Pecan Preserve

1 kg (2¼ lb) ripe firm
   peaches
450 g (1 lb) Sugar with
   Pectin
juice of 1 lemon
150 ml (¼ pint) Bourbon
2 tablespoons fresh mint,
   chopped
85 g (3 oz) shelled pecans,
   chopped

Quantity: 1.5 litres
   (2½ pints)
Storage: refrigerated,
   6 weeks
   frozen, 6 months

Bring a small deep saucepan of water to the boil. Drop one peach at a time into the simmering water; count to 5 and remove the peach with a slotted spoon. Then peel off the skin. When all the peaches are peeled, cut the peaches in half and remove the stones. Place the peach halves in a saucepan and mash them with a potato masher. Add the sugar and lemon juice to the mashed peaches and stir over a low heat until the sugar is dissolved. Raise the heat and bring to the boil. Boil hard for 4–5 minutes until the jam has set. Remove from the heat and stir in the Bourbon, mint and pecans. Ladle into sterilised jars, cover, and seal at once.

Carrot, Orange and Cardamom Jam

1 kg (2¼ lb) carrots
grated zest and juice of
*   2 oranges*
500 g (17 oz) Sugar with
*   Pectin*
500 g (17 oz) preserving
*   sugar*
6 green cardamom pods,
*   crushed*
juice of 1 lemon

Quantity: 1.75 litres
*   (6 pints)*
Storage: vacuum-sealed,
*   1 year*

Scrape or peel the carrots. Then cut them into thin slices and boil until tender in just enough water to prevent them burning. Drain the carrots, reserving any cooking water. Purée the carrots in a food processor and turn them into a large saucepan or preserving pan. Add the cooking water, orange zest and juice, both sugars and the cardamom pods tied in a muslin bag. Stir carefully over a moderate heat until the sugar is dissolved. Then simmer, stirring fairly often until the jam sets. Remove from the heat, fish out the cardamom bag and add the lemon juice. Ladle into hot, sterilised jars, cover, and seal at once.

IN INDIA, CARROT pudding is a favourite dessert, and is made by hours of simmering and stirring a mixture of carrots, milk, spices and sugar until it has an almost jam-like consistency. This jam is reminiscent in flavour, but is not as arduous to prepare.

Carrot, Orange and Cardamom Jam;
Peach Confiture with Armagnac

Peach Confiture with Armagnac

1 kg (2¼ lb) firm ripe
  peaches
juice of 1 lemon
300 ml (½ pint) Armagnac
520 g (1 lb 2 oz) Sugar with
  Pectin

Quantity: 1.2 litres (2 pints)
Storage: refrigerated,
  6 weeks
    frozen, 6 months

Bring a small deep saucepan filled with water to the boil. Drop one peach at a time into the simmering water; count to 5, lift out the peach and peel off the skin. When all the peaches are peeled, remove the stones and chop the flesh coarsely. Place the chopped peaches in a bowl with the lemon juice, half the Armagnac and the sugar. Cover and leave at room temperature for 12 hours.

DRAIN THE SYRUP from the peaches into a saucepan. Bring to the boil and boil for 5 minutes. Add the peaches, return to the boil and cook until thick. Stir in the remaining Armagnac, ladle into the sterilised jars, cover, and seal at once. Cool before placing in the refrigerator.

Nectarine and Passion-fruit Jam

4 firm ripe nectarines

4 passion-fruit

225 g (8 oz) Sugar with
  Pectin

3 tablespoons fresh lemon
  juice

Quantity: approx 600 ml
  (1 pint)

Storage: refrigerated,
  8 weeks
  frozen, 6 months

Bring a small deep saucepan filled with water to the boil. Drop one nectarine at a time into the simmering water, lifting the fruit out after 4–5 seconds. Peel off the skin, halve and pit. Chop the flesh into very small pieces and place in a heavy-bottomed saucepan. (Alternatively, you can slice the fruit into the pan and mash with a potato masher). Cut the passion-fruit in half, scoop out the insides with a teaspoon and place in a blender. Blend at a low speed for a minute to detatch the membranes from the seeds. Sieve over the saucepan on to the nectarines. Add the sugar and lemon juice. Bring to the boil, stirring occasionally until the sugar is dissolved. Boil for 3–4 minutes.

Remove from the heat and put in sterilised jars. Cover and seal at once.

THE SUBLIME SWEET yet sharp flavour of passion-fruit works miracles for this nectarine jam. Passion-fruit act like exotic lemons and bring out the flavour of other fruit. Try this jam with plain yogurt or use it to sandwich a sponge cake for a special occasion.

F i g   a n d   B r a n d y   J a m

450 g (1 lb) fresh ripe figs
3 tablespoons water
⅛ teaspoon ground
*   cinnamon*
225 g (8 oz) Sugar with
*   Pectin*
juice of 1 lemon
4 tablespoons brandy

Quantity: 600 ml (1 pint)
Storage: vacuum-sealed,
*   1 year*

Carefully peel the figs and then quarter them. Place them in a saucepan with the water, cinnamon, sugar and lemon juice. Bring slowly to the boil, stirring frequently. Then increase the heat and boil for several minutes, until the jam is thick. Remove from the heat and stir in the brandy. Ladle into hot, sterilised jars, cover, and seal at once.

A DELICIOUS SPREAD and an excellent filling for cookies or cakes.

D a t e   a n d   B r a n d y   C o n s e r v e

340 g (12 oz) dates,
*   chopped*
170 g (6 oz) currants
100 g (3½ oz) brown sugar
¼ teaspoon grated lemon
*   zest*
juice of 1 lemon
150 ml (¼ pint) fresh
*   orange juice*
60 g (2 oz) walnuts,
*   chopped*
150 ml (¼ pint) brandy

Quantity: 600 ml (1 pint)
Storage: vacuum-sealed,
*   1 year*

Combine the dates, currants, brown sugar, lemon zest, lemon juice and orange juice in a heavy saucepan. Stir over a medium heat until the mixture comes to the boil. Then boil for 5 minutes, continually stirring until thick. Remove from the heat and add the walnuts and brandy. Pour into hot, sterilised jars, cover and seal at once.

A WONDERFUL FILLING for mince pies.

Strawberry and Rum Preserve

1 kg (2¼ lb) firm, ripe
   strawberries
juice and finely grated zest
   from 1 small lemon
150 ml (¼ pint) water
680 g (1½ lb) Sugar with
   Pectin
3 tablespoons white rum

Quantity: 900 ml
   (1½ pints)
Storage: vacuum-sealed,
   1 year

Hull the strawberries and wipe any that are gritty. Do not wash them unless it is absolutely necessary. Place them in a bowl and sprinkle with the lemon juice and zest.

Carefully bring the water and sugar to the boil, and boil for 4 minutes. Pour over the strawberries and leave for 1 hour.

Turn the strawberries and syrup into a preserving pan, bring slowly to the boil, and then boil rapidly until the setting point is reached. Remove from the heat and stir in the rum. Ladle into hot, sterilised jars, cover and seal at once.

Plum, Walnut and Brandy Conserve

120 g (4 oz) walnut halves
1 kg (2¼ lb) greengage or
   other full-flavoured
   plums
juice of 1 lemon
150 ml (¼ pint) water
450 g (1 lb) Sugar with
   Pectin
4 tablespoons brandy

Quantity: 1.2 litres
   (2 pints)
Storage: refrigerated,
   3 months
   frozen, 6 months

Toast the walnuts in a small, heavy frying pan for 5 minutes. Cool the walnuts and chop coarsely. Wash, quarter and stone the plums. Place them in a saucepan or small preserving pan with the lemon juice and water. Simmer, covered, until the plums are soft. Add the sugar, and 2 tablespoons of the brandy. Dissolve the sugar over a low heat. Then bring to the boil and boil for 4–5 minutes until the jam has set. Remove from the heat and add the walnuts and remaining brandy. Ladle into sterilised jars, cover and seal at once. Refrigerate when cool.

Gooseberry and Elderflower Jam

1.8 kg (4 lb) firm green
  gooseberries
900 ml (1½ pints) water
1.8 kg (4 lb) preserving or
  granulated sugar
8–10 heads of elderflowers

Quantity: 2.25 litres
  (4 pints)
Storage: vacuum-sealed,
  1 year

Top and tail the gooseberries and place them with the water in a preserving pan. Cook gently for 30 minutes, or until the skins are tender.

Meanwhile, warm the sugar in a very low oven. Place the elderflowers in a square of muslin and tie into a bag; then add to the soft gooseberries. Cook over a medium heat until the sugar has dissolved. Then raise the heat and boil hard until the jam sets. (Gooseberries are high in pectin so test after 5 minutes.) Remove the elderflower bag, squeezing the juices back into the pan. Ladle into hot, sterilised jars, cover, and seal at once.

A LOVELY AND very easy jam to make in June when both elderflowers and gooseberries are in season. The elderflower blossoms impart a delicate muscat grape flavour to the jam.

Chestnut and Armagnac Preserve

1 kg (2¼ lb) chestnuts
680 g (1½ lb) granulated
sugar
grated zest from half a
lemon
150 ml (¼ pint) water
8 tablespoons Armagnac

Quantity: approx 1.2 litres
(2 pints)
Storage: refrigerated,
3 months
frozen, 6 months

To peel the chestnuts, cut a cross through the skin of each chestnut. Place a few at a time in boiling water and boil for 3–4 minutes. Then, using rubber gloves, peel off both inner and outer skins while the chestnuts are still very hot. Alternatively, place them in a microwave oven after they have been nicked, and give them a few minutes on high, before peeling them. Place the peeled chestnuts in a preserving pan with the sugar, lemon zest and water. Simmer gently, stirring, until the chestnuts have turned into a thick-textured purée. Remove from the heat and stir in the Armagnac. Place in warm, sterilised jars, cover, and seal at once. Refrigerate or freeze when cool.

K i w i   L i m e   C o n s e r v e

580 g (1¼ lb) ripe kiwi-
fruit
juice of 2 large limes
300 g (10 oz) Sugar with
Pectin

Quantity: 600 ml (1 pint)
Storage: refrigerated,
4 weeks
frozen, 6 months

Peel the kiwi-fruit with a potato peeler. Then cut each fruit first into quarters and then into small dice. Place these in a heavy-bottomed saucepan with the lime juice. Add the sugar and bring slowly to the boil. Boil hard for 4 minutes. Then ladle into sterilised jars, cover, and seal at once. Refrigerate when cool.

SLICING OPEN AN unpromising-looking kiwi-fruit for the first time is a revelation. The enchanting green and black sunray pattern is an unexpected surprise. The fruit also has a refreshing flavour and is very high in vitamin C and low in calories. This conserve is beautiful to look at and delicate enough to be used for special tarts, or perfect to serve with a coeur de crème, petit-suisse, or plain yogurt.

K i w i   a n d   T a m a r i l l o   P r e s e r v e

6 ripe kiwi-fruit
6 ripe tamarillo
Sugar with Pectin

Quantity: 450 ml (¾ pint)
Storage: refrigerated,
4 weeks
frozen, 6 months

Peel off the thin layer of brown skin from the kiwi-fruit and dice the flesh. Scoop out the flesh of the halved tamarillos and chop it roughly. Weigh the two together and turn them into a heavy-bottomed saucepan. Add half the weight of sugar to the fruit. Bring to the boil. Then boil hard for 4 minutes before putting in sterilised jars, covering, and sealing.

Kiwi and Tamarillo Preserve;
Kiwi Lime Conserve;
Greengage and Almond Conserve

Greengage and Almond Conserve

925 g (2 lb) greengage
   plums
juice and grated zest of
   1 lemon
450 g (1 lb) Sugar with
   Pectin
120 g (4 oz) slivered
   almonds, toasted
8 tablespoons Mirabelle or
   other plum liqueur

Quantity: 1.2 litres
   (2 pints)
Storage: refrigerated,
   6 months
   frozen, 1 year

Wash the plums and then halve and stone them. Chop the plums into small pieces.

Place the chopped plums and lemon juice in a pan over a low heat and cook, stirring, until the plums are soft. Add the sugar, and bring to the boil, stirring to dissolve the sugar. Then boil hard for 3–4 minutes. Remove from the heat and stir in the lemon zest, almonds and liqueur. Put into sterilised jars, cover, and seal at once. Refrigerate when the conserve is cool.

F l a v o u r e d   S u g a r s

Vanilla Sugar: This is the most well-known of the flavoured sugars. Store several vanilla pods in an air-tight jar of caster sugar and use this to replace some or all of the sugar in your recipe.

Lavender Sugar: Pick the flower heads of lavender just before they come into bloom. Strip off the individual flowers and lay them on a lined tray to dry for 24 hours. Weigh the flowers and add 6 times their volume of granulated sugar. Grind together in a clean coffee grinder or small blender. Spread out again to dry for several hours. Then store in air-tight jars. Use sparingly.

Mint Sugar: Apple or pineapple mint varieties are excellent for flavouring sugars. Follow the method for lavender sugar.

Rose Petal Sugar: This is made in much the same way as lavender sugar. Use red fragrant roses and cut off the white ends of the petals. Dry them overnight and grind them with 5 times their weight of sugar.

FLAVOURED SUGARS CAN be used for any number of desserts, including ice creams and cakes, as well as custards and puddings. They can be stored for an indefinite time in air-tight jars.

J a m a i c a n   J a m

3 limes
1 kg (2¼ lb) ripe, sound
bananas (peeled weight)
750 g (1 lb 10 oz) caster
sugar
¼ grated nutmeg
150 ml (¼ pint) rum

Quantity: 1.5 litres
(2½ pints)
Storage: refrigerated,
3 months
frozen, 6 months

Peel the zest from the limes (without the pith) and cut into very thin strips. Blanch in boiling water for 8 minutes. Strain into a sieve and refresh under cold running water. Then drain and set aside. Squeeze the juice from the limes. Mash the bananas with the lime juice, then turn into a large saucepan and add the sugar. Stir with a wooden spoon over a very low heat until the sugar is dissolved. Add the lime zest and boil the jam for about 30 minutes, stirring continually, until the jam is thick.

Remove from the heat and stir in the nutmeg and rum. Reduce the quantity of rum accordingly if you are potting some without alcohol. Put the jam into sterilised jars, cover, and seal at once. Store the jam in the refrigerator.

YOU MIGHT WANT to consider adding rum to only half the jam so that you can use some for the family breakfast and the rum half for evening desserts. It is delicious with fromage frais or with waffles or crêpes.

Pineapple Kiwi Jam with Kirsch

*3 kiwi-fruit, peeled and cut
   into chunks*
*925 g (2 lb) fresh pineapple
   (weighed after pineapple
   has been cored and
   peeled)*
*580 g (1 ¼ lb) Sugar with
   Pectin*
8 tablespoons Kirsch

*Quantity: 1.75 litres
   (3 pints)*
*Storage: vacuum-sealed,
   1 year*

Place the kiwi-fruit and pineapple in a food processor and blend to a purée. Turn into a preserving pan or large saucepan. Add the sugar and stir over moderate heat until the sugar is dissolved. Raise the heat and bring to a rolling boil. Boil for about 4–5 minutes, or until the jam has set. Remove from the heat. Stir in the Kirsch and put immediately into warmed, sterilised jars. Cover and seal at once.

Blackberry Calvados Jam

225 g (8 oz) cooking apples
450 g (1 lb) blackberries
juice of 1 lemon
340 g (12 oz) Sugar with
  Pectin
6 tablespoons Calvados

Quantity: 900 ml
  (1½ pints)
Storage: vacuum-sealed,
  1 year

Peel, core and grate the apples. Place them in a saucepan with the blackberries and lemon juice. Cook over a gentle heat, stirring, until the fruit is soft.

Then add the sugar and half the Calvados and stir until the sugar has dissolved. Bring to a rolling boil and cook rapidly for about 4–5 minutes until the jam has set. Remove from the heat and add the rest of the Calvados. Put into sterilised jars, cover, and seal at once.

R o s e   P e t a l   J a m

450 g (1 lb) scented rose
  petals
450 g (1 lb) Sugar with
  Pectin
600 ml (1 pint) water
juice of 1 lemon
1 teaspoon rose water
  (optional)

Quantity: 600 ml (1 pint)
Storage: vacuum-sealed,
  1 year

Snip off and discard the white bases of the rose flowers. Snip the petals into irregular pieces. Place them in a bowl and mix with half the sugar. Cover and leave for 24 hours. Place the rose petals, water, lemon juice and remaining sugar in a small preserving pan or heavy-bottomed saucepan. Bring to the boil and boil rapidly for about 5 minutes until the jam has set. Stir in the rose water if using this. Then put in sterilised jars, cover, and seal at once.

ROSES SMELL GOOD enough to eat and they are edible, not only in lovely jams such as this, but also scattered over salads or crystallised for decorative uses. Rose petal jam is one of the most delicate and sublime of all jams. A spoonful is delicious added to hot tea. You will need a scented rose, such as Zephirine Drouhin, or any of the rugosas.

Blueberry Apple Conserve;
Uncooked Raspberry Jam;
Rose Petal Jam

Uncooked Raspberry Jam

925 g (2 lb) dry raspberries
925 g (2 lb) caster sugar

Quantity: 1.2 litres (2 pints)
Storage: refrigerated,
   3 months
   frozen, 6 months

Put the raspberries in one shallow bowl and the sugar in another. Place both in an oven heated to Gas Mark 3/160°C/325°F and allow to heat through for about 10–15 minutes without letting the sugar colour.

Remove from the oven. Add the raspberries to the sugar and stir for about 10 minutes until the sugar has dissolved. Put into sterilised jars, cover and seal at once. Store, when cool, in the refrigerator or freezer.

ONLY DRY FRUIT is suitable for this method of making jam. The result is one of the best jams imaginable.

Blueberry Apple Conserve

225 g (8 oz) cooking apples
450 g (1 lb) blueberries
1 bay leaf
juice and grated zest of
   1 lemon
450 g (1 lb) Sugar with
   Pectin

Quantity: 900 ml
   (1½ pints)
Storage: vacuum-sealed,
   1 year

Peel, core and grate the apples. Place them, the blueberries, bay leaf, lemon zest and juice in a heavy saucepan or small preserving pan and cook gently, stirring to soften the fruit. Add the sugar and stir until the sugar has dissolved. Then bring to the boil and boil hard for 5 minutes, or until the jam has set. Pour immediately into warmed, sterilised jars, cover, and seal at once.

R h u b a r b   a n d   G i n g e r   J a m

1.3 kg (3 lb) young rhubarb
450 g (1 lb) cooking apples,
  peeled, cored and sliced
1.3 kg (3 lb) granulated
  sugar
juice of 2 lemons
2.5 cm (1-inch) piece of
  fresh ginger, peeled and
  chopped finely
60 g (2 oz) preserved or
  crystallised ginger,
  chopped
grated zest of 1 orange

Quantity: approx 2.5 litres
  (2½ pints)
Storage: vacuum-sealed,
  1 year

Wipe the rhubarb clean and cut it into small pieces. Place these in a bowl with the apple slices, sugar, lemon juice, both gingers and the orange zest. Cover and leave overnight. The next day, place in a non-aluminium preserving pan and bring slowly to the boil. Stir to dissolve the sugar. Boil rapidly for about 15–20 minutes until set. Then put into sterilised jars, cover, and seal at once.

THIS IS BEST made in the spring when the rhubarb is young and tender and a lovely pink colour.

C r a n b e r r y   P i n e a p p l e   P r e s e r v e

120 g (4 oz) dried apricots
225 g (8 oz) fresh
  cranberries
300 g (10 oz) can of
  crushed pineapple
340 g (12 oz) Sugar with
  Pectin.

Quantity: 1 litre (1¾ pints)
Storage: vacuum-sealed,
  6 months

Soak the apricots overnight in sufficient water to cover them.

Drain, chop and combine the apricots with the cranberries and pineapple in a heavy-bottomed saucepan. Heat the mixture to a simmer, stir in the sugar and boil for 4 minutes. Remove from the heat, pour into sterilised jars, cover, and seal at once.

C a p e   G o o s e b e r r y   –   P h y s a l i s   –   J a m

225 g (8 oz) cape
*   gooseberries*
2 tablespoons lemon juice
2 tablespoons water
200 g (7 oz) Sugar with
*   Pectin*

Quantity: 300 ml (½ pint)
Storage: vacuum-sealed,
*   1 year*

Remove the dry, thin calyx and prick each berry with a needle. Place the berries in a saucepan with the lemon juice and water. Simmer very gently, covered, for 5 minutes or until the fruit has softened. Add the sugar and stir over a low heat until dissolved. Then boil rapidly for 4–5 minutes until the setting point has been reached. Pour into a hot, sterilised jar, cover, and seal at once.

YOU ARE MOST likely to come across the cape gooseberry on a plate of petits fours, with the delicate calyx folded back like wings and the orange berry coated in shiny white fondant. With their sharp flavour and pretty orange colour they make a very special jam. The familiar orange Chinese Lanterns are a member of the same family. (In fact the berry inside the lantern is edible, but it is too dry and small to be worth bothering with.)

Melon and Ginger Jam;
Cape Gooseberry–Physalis–Jam;
Mango Lime and Rum Jam

Melon and Ginger Jam

450 g (1 lb) slightly under-
   ripe cantaloupe melon
   flesh (weighed after
   peeling and removing
   seeds)
finely grated zest and juice
   of 2 limes
a 2.5 cm (1-inch) piece of
   fresh ginger, peeled, then
   chopped
60 g (2 oz) preserved stem
   ginger, drained, then
   chopped
340 g (12 oz) Sugar with
   Pectin

Quantity: 900 ml
   (1½ pints)
Storage: vacuum-sealed,
   1 year

Cut the melon flesh into cubes. Place the melon cubes in a pan with the lime zest and juice and ginger. Simmer gently for a few minutes to soften the melon. Add the sugar and stir until the sugar has dissolved. Then bring to a rolling boil and boil for about 8 minutes until set. Put into sterilised jars, cover, and seal at once.

Dried Apricot Jam with Curaçao

340 g (12 oz) dried apricots
1.75 litres (3 pints) boiling
  water
450 g (1 lb) Sugar with
  Pectin
juice of 2 lemons
4 tablespoons Curaçao or
  Grand Marnier
120 g (4 oz) flaked almonds

Quantity: 1.2 litres (2 pints)
Storage: vacuum-sealed,
  1 year

Wash the fruit, place them in a large bowl and pour over the boiling water. Leave for 1–3 days until the fruit are swollen and soft. Turn them into a preserving pan and simmer until tender. Add extra water if the apricots look too dry. When the fruit is soft, break up with a potato masher leaving some chunks. Add the sugar and bring the fruit back to a simmer. Stir in the lemon juice and almonds and boil for about 5 minutes until set. Add the Curaçao. Then ladle into sterilised jars, cover, and seal at once.

Mango Lime and Rum Jam

2 slightly under-ripe
  mangoes
juice of 1 lime
Sugar with Pectin
4–5 tablespoons rum

Quantity: 600 ml (1 pint)
Storage: vacuum-sealed,
  6 months
  refrigerated, 9 months

Peel the skin from the mangoes with a potato peeler. Slice off the flesh in lengthwise sections. You should have about 280 g (10 oz). For this amount use 200 g (7 oz) of Sugar with Pectin. For 230 g (8 oz) of mango use 150 g (5 oz) of Sugar with Pectin. Purée the mango and lime juice in a food processor or blender. Pour into a saucepan and add the sugar. Heat gently, stirring continuously, until the sugar is dissolved. Then bring to a rolling boil and boil for 3–4 minutes or until set. Remove from the heat and stir in the rum. Put into sterilised jars, cover, and seal at once.

EATING A FRESH ripe mango is an unbeatable treat, but a good mango jam is a close second.

H o n e y   A m b r o s i a

120 g (4 oz) seeded raisins,
*   chopped*
45 g (1½ oz) dried apricots,
*   chopped*
60 g (2 oz) almonds,
*   chopped*
60 g (2 oz) shelled pecans,
*   chopped*
2 tablespoons rum or
*   brandy*
2 × 450 g (1 lb) jars of
*   clear honey*

Quantity: 1.40 kg (3 lb)
Storage: in an air-tight jar,
*   1 year*

Mix the raisins, apricots and nuts in a bowl. Stir in the rum or brandy, cover, and leave overnight. The next day empty the honey into a bowl. Mix in the fruit, nuts and brandy and ladle into 3 airtight jars.

Two pots of honey can be turned into three extra-special ones by adding fruit and nuts. This is very good on yogurt or as a spread on bread or toast. Use the larger seeded raisins, as these come from better tasting varieties than the seedless raisins.

L a v e n d e r   H o n e y

450 g (1 lb) honey
1 teacup lavender flower
*   heads, just coming into*
*   bloom*

Quantity: approx 450 g
*   (1 lb)*
Storage: in an air-tight jar,
*   9 months*

Heat the honey with the lavender heads gently to just below simmering point. Remove from the heat, cover, and leave to infuse for an hour. Reheat again to a bare simmer. Then pour through a strainer into small sterilised jars. Seal with tightly-fitting lids. Store for 2 weeks before using.

THE FLAVOUR of a dull honey can be greatly improved with lavender.

Honey Ambrosia;
Candied Pomelo Peel

Candied Pomelo Peel

1 large pomelo
340 g (12 oz) granulated
sugar, plus extra for
coating
water

Quantity: 575 g (1¼ lb)
Storage: in an air-tight jar,
1 year

Make cuts through the pomelo skin and pith lengthwise in about 8 sections. Peel away the sections, removing both pith and skin. Then cut these into thin slices. Cover the peel with a good quantity of water. Bring to the boil and boil for 5 minutes. Then drain and rinse under cold water. Repeat this twice more but the last (third) time simmer the peel until it is tender. Drain and set aside. Place the sugar in a heap in the centre of a heavy saucepan. Pour 250 ml (8 fl oz) of water around the sugar and heat carefully until the sugar is dissolved. Add the peel, bring to a boil and simmer until the syrup has practically disappeared; this can take about 30 minutes. Spread a layer of sugar on a tray lined with baking parchment. Lift the peel with a fork on to the paper. When cool, sprinkle with more sugar. When completely cold, spread the sugared peel out on a rack and place in a dry, warm place until dry. Store in an air-tight jar.

ANY CITRUS FRUIT can be candied like this.

Honey Butter

120 g (4 oz) butter
150 ml (¼ pint) honey

Quantity: approx 225 g
(8 oz)
Storage: refrigerated,
6 weeks

Cream the butter and slowly mix in the honey. Store in an air-tight jar.

THIS IS ANOTHER handy spread.

Papaya and Lime Preserve

2 ripe papayas
150 ml (¼ pint) fresh lime
* juice (about 2 limes)*
170 g (6 oz) Sugar with
* Pectin*

Quantity: approx 600 ml
* (1 pint)*
Storage: refrigerated,
* 3 months*
*   frozen, 6 months*

Cut each papaya in half lengthwise. Remove the seeds with a spoon and discard. Cut off the skin and any unripe flesh under the skin. Slice the ripe flesh. You should have about 425 g (14 oz). Place in a saucepan with the lime juice and mash with a potato masher. Add the sugar and bring slowly to the boil. Boil for 3 minutes. Then pour into warm, sterilised jars, cover, and seal at once. Keep refrigerated when cool.

IN INDIA, WEDGES of lime are served with large apricot-pink slices of papaya for breakfast. The lime juice transforms the sometimes mild-tasting papaya. The two papayas needed for this jam will give many mornings a special, exotic beginning. The papayas available here are a smaller variety than their Indian cousin. They are ripe when the skin has largely turned yellow.

S h a r o n   a n d   P a s s i o n - f r u i t
P r e s e r v e

3 slightly soft sharon-fruit
    (skins should be mottled
    with some brown)
1 passion-fruit
juice of 1 lime
340 g (12 oz) Sugar with
    Pectin

Quantity: 450 ml (¾ pint)
Storage: vacuum-sealed,
    6 months

Wash the sharon-fruit and remove the stems. Quarter the fruit and place in a food processor. Process until the fruit is finely chopped and then turn into a saucepan.

Cut the passion-fruit in half. Scoop out the flesh and add it to the pan along with the lime juice. Bring the fruit gently to a simmer, add the sugar, and stir until the sugar has dissolved. Raise the heat and bring to the boil. Then boil for 4–5 minutes until the mixture thickens. Ladle into sterilised jars, cover, and seal at once.

SHARON-FRUIT, A hybrid persimmon developed in Israel, has an advantage over the persimmon in that it can be eaten skin and all when the fruit is still firm. Persimmons, on the other hand, have to be eaten when they are very soft and ripe; but then they offer a luscious perfumed flesh that no sharon-fruit can match. Both fruits can be used for this preserve but persimmons must be skinned first.

Sharon and Passion-fruit Preserve;
Papaya and Lime Preserve;
Black Forest Preserve

Black Forest Preserve

1.2 kg (2½ lb) black
   cherries, stoned
juice of 2 lemons
1.3 kg (3 lb) Sugar with
   Pectin
8 tablespoons Kirsch

Quantity: 1.5 litres
   (2½ pints)
Storage: vacuum-sealed,
   1 year

Place the prepared cherries in a pan with the lemon juice and sugar. Bring slowly to the boil, stirring, until the sugar has dissolved. Then boil hard for about 5 minutes until the setting point is reached. Add the Kirsch and pour into hot, sterilised jars. Cover and seal at once.

Cranberry Orange Conserve

450 g (1 lb) cranberries
150 ml (¼ pint) water
120 g (4 oz) raisins
450 g (1 lb) granulated
   sugar
grated zest from 1 large
   orange
300 ml (½ pint) fresh
   orange juice
120 g (4 oz) pecans or
   walnuts, chopped
2 tablespoons Curaçao or
   Grand Marnier

Quantity: 1.2 litres
   (2 pints)
Storage: vacuum-sealed,
   1 year

Place the cranberries in a saucepan with the water. Simmer gently, covered, until the fruit skins break. Sieve and return to a clean pan. Add the raisins, sugar, orange zest and juice and bring to the boil over a medium heat. Raise the heat and boil, stirring occasionally, until the mixture thickens. Remove from the heat and stir in the nuts and liqueur. Pour into hot, sterilised jars, cover, and seal at once.

THIS BRIGHT RED cranberry conserve is sharp enough to go well with meats or game. It is also good as a filling for tartlets, or can be added to apple pies for extra flavour.

G r e n a d a   P i n a   C o l a d a   J a m

225 g (8 oz) fresh pineapple
(weighed after being
peeled and cored)
5 tablespoons fresh or
bought coconut cream
1 tablespoon lemon juice
120 g (4 oz) Sugar with
Pectin

Quantity: 450 ml (¾ pint)
Storage: refrigerated,
4 months
frozen, 6 months

Purée the pineapple and coconut cream in a food processor. Pour the mixture into a non-aluminium saucepan and add the lemon juice and sugar. Stir over a gentle heat to dissolve the sugar. Then bring to the boil and boil for about 3–4 minutes. Pour into a hot, sterilised jar and seal. Refrigerate when cold.

Note: To make the coconut cream: break a coconut by using the blunt end of a heavy cleaver and hitting it around the circumference of the coconut. Hold the coconut on a hard surface while you are doing this. When the coconut cracks, pour the coconut water into a bowl. This can be filtered and drunk if desired. Pry out the coconut meat and pare off the brown skin with a potato peeler. Grate 230 g (8 oz) of the coconut meat and place in a blender. Pour about 300 ml (½ pint) of hot water over the grated coconut and blend for 5 minutes. Leave for 30 minutes, then strain through a triple thickness of muslin, squeezing out as much liquid as possible. This liquid is called coconut milk. Place the coconut milk in a glass container and refrigerate for 20 minutes. The coconut cream will rise to the top and can be skimmed off.

A VACATION IN Grenada inspired this jam. A Grenada pina colada is a pina colada minus the rum. To my delight this jam tastes surprisingly like this delicious drink.

Onion Jam

100 g (3½ oz) butter
1 tablespoon olive oil
925 g (2 lb) onions,
  chopped
2 teaspoons salt
freshly ground black pepper
170 g (6 oz) caster sugar
8 tablespoons raspberry
  vinegar
300 ml (½ pint) red wine

Quantity: 600 ml (1 pint)
Storage: refrigerated,
  6 weeks

Heat the butter and olive oil in a large sauté pan until it is bubbling hot. Then stir in the onions, salt, pepper and sugar. Cover the pan and simmer very gently for about 40 minutes, stirring occasionally. Uncover the pan and add the vinegar and wine. Simmer, uncovered, for another 30 minutes or until the onions have absorbed all the liquid and are a jam-like consistency. Keep an eye on them towards the end of the cooking time and stir often to prevent scorching. Spoon into sterilised jars, cover, and seal at once.

MY FAVOURITE COMPOTE to serve with pâtés, terrines and cold meats, this is also delicious hot used as a filling for tiny tarts to serve as an hors d'oeuvre.

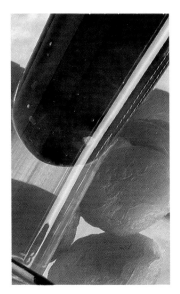

There is in every cook's opinion
No savoury dish without an onion;
But lest your kissing should be spoiled
The onion must be thoroughly boiled
Jonathan Swift

c h u t n e y s

Mango Chutney

1 kg (2¼ lb) green unripe
   mangoes
225 g (8 oz) sultanas
120 g (4 oz) cashew nuts,
   chopped
60 g (2 oz) fresh ginger,
   peeled and chopped finely
2 garlic cloves, peeled and
   chopped finely
2 chillies, de-seeded and
   chopped
450 g (1 lb) light-brown
   sugar
450 ml (¾ pint) cider
   vinegar

Quantity: 1.2 litres (2 pints)
Storage: vacuum-packed,
   2 years

Peel the mangoes. Then cut off all the flesh and chop it into small cubes. Place these in a non-aluminium preserving pan with the other ingredients. Bring slowly to a boil, stirring, and then simmer gently for about 30 minutes until thick. Ladle into hot, sterilised jars and cover at once. Seal with non-metallic lids or Cellophane. Store for 6 weeks before using.

Plum and Ginger Chutney

450 g (1 lb) eating apples,
  peeled and cored
2 medium-size onions,
  peeled and sliced
1.3 kg (3 lb) damson or
  other cooking plums,
  stoned
225 g (8 oz) sultanas
85 g (3 oz) crystallised or
  peeled fresh ginger,
  chopped finely
1 fresh chilli, de-seeded and
  chopped
1 teaspoon ground allspice
600 ml (1 pint) cider
  vinegar
225 g (8 oz) demerara
  sugar

Quantity: 1.2 litres (2 pints)
Storage: vacuum-sealed,
  2 years

Place all the ingredients in a large non-aluminium preserving pan. Heat gently, stirring, until the sugar is dissolved. Then simmer gently until the chutney is thick – about 1 hour. Ladle into sterilised jars and cover at once. Seal with non-metallic lids or Cellophane. Store for 6 weeks before using.

THIS IS A wonderful way to use up excess plums, particularly damsons which give such a good sharp flavour to chutneys.

Honeydew Chutney with Brandy

1 good-sized honeydew
   melon
water
salt
450 ml (¾ pint) cider
   vinegar
400 g (14 oz) light-brown
   sugar
1 teaspoon ground ginger
1 dried chilli, crumbled
1 teaspoon allspice berries,
   crushed
5 cm (2-inch) stick of
   cinnamon
1 medium-size onion,
   chopped
1 garlic clove, chopped
85 g (3 oz) currants
6 tablespoons brandy or
   Cognac

Quantity: approx 1.2 litres
   (2 pints)
Storage: vacuum-sealed,
   1 year

Halve the melon and remove the seeds. Cut the melon into wedges. Then cut out the flesh and cut into 2.5 cm (1-inch) cubes. Place them in a bowl, cover with cold water and stir in 3 tablespoons of salt. Cover and refrigerate overnight. The next day drain the melon and rinse under cold running water. Use a non-aluminium preserving or heavy saucepan and put in it the vinegar, sugar, ginger, chilli, allspice berries, cinnamon and ½ teaspoon of salt. Bring to a boil and then add the melon, onion, garlic and currants. Simmer for about 1½ hours until the mixture has reduced in volume and has thickened.

Then stir in the brandy. Spoon into sterilised warm jars, cover and seal at once with non-metallic lids or Cellophane. Store in a cool place for 6 weeks before using.

A p r i c o t a n d W a l n u t C h u t n e y

450 g (1 lb) dried apricots
1 China-tea bag
water
1 kg (2¼ lb) onions, sliced
finely
225 g (8 oz) sultanas
600 ml (1 pint) cider
vinegar
450 g (1 lb) muscavado
sugar
1 teaspoon salt
60 g (2 oz) fresh ginger,
peeled and chopped
2 teaspoons black mustard
seeds
1 dried or fresh chilli,
de-seeded if fresh, and
chopped
grated zest and juice from
1 orange
140 g (5 oz) walnuts,
chopped

Quantity: 1.2 litres (2 pints)
Storage: vacuum-sealed,
2 years

Place the apricots and tea bag in a bowl and cover with boiling water; leave overnight to soak. The next day discard the tea bag and place the apricots and the soaking liquid in a large non-aluminium saucepan. Add all the rest of the ingredients except the walnuts. Bring to a simmer, stirring, and then simmer gently for about 1½ hours until the mixture thickens. Remove from the heat and add the walnuts. Ladle into warm, sterilised jars and cover immediately. Seal with non-metallic lids or Cellophane. Store for 6 weeks before using.

LOOK FOR SLIGHTLY shrivelled dried apricot halves, rather than the plumped-up whole ones. Such apricots look less appealing but have a much better flavour and make all the difference in preserves.

Elderberry and Apple Chutney

450 g (1 lb) elderberries
1.3 kg (3 lb) cooking or
    windfall apples, peeled
    and cored
225 g (8 oz) raisins
60 g (2 oz) fresh ginger,
    grated
2 dried chillies, chopped
a stick of cinnamon
a good pinch of ground
    cloves
900 ml (1½ pints) cider
    vinegar
680 g (1½ lb) demerara
    sugar

Quantity: 1.5 litres
    (2½ pints)
Storage: vacuum-sealed,
    2 years

Take the stems off the elderberries by using the prongs of a fork. Slice the apples and add them, along with the elderberries and the rest of the ingredients, to a large non-aluminium pan. Heat gently, stirring, until the sugar is dissolved and then bring to a boil. Simmer gently for about 1 hour, stirring occasionally, until the chutney thickens. Ladle into sterilised jars and cover at once, sealing with non-metallic lids or Cellophane. Store for at least 8 weeks before using.

IT IS NICE to find ways of using free food and this is an excellent way of enjoying elderberries. If you can find windfall apples as well, your chutney will be a real gift!

Spiced Kumquats

1.3 kg (3 lb) kumquats
water
925 g (2 lb) sugar
1 stick of cinnamon
1½ tablespoons cloves
6 blades of mace
4 cardamom pods
600 ml (1 pint) cider
  vinegar

Quantity: 900 ml
  (1½ pints)
Storage: vacuum-sealed,
  1 year

Place the kumquats in a non-aluminium saucepan, barely covering them with water. Cover the pan and simmer very gently for about 15 minutes. Meanwhile, dissolve the sugar and spices in the vinegar over a gentle heat. Bring to a boil and boil the syrup for 5 minutes. Drain the kumquats, reserving the liquid. Place the kumquats in the syrup, adding the reserved liquid to cover the fruit if necessary. Simmer for 30 minutes. Remove the pan from the heat and leave uncovered for 24 hours, turning the fruit occasionally in the syrup. The next day bring the kumquats and syrup to the boil. Drain the fruit and pack into sterilised jars. Bring the syrup back to the boil and boil hard to thicken slightly. Pour the syrup over the kumquats, distributing the spices between the jars, cover, and seal at once with non-metallic lids or Cellophane. Store for about 6 weeks before using.

THESE ARE PARTICULARLY good with ham, tongue, turkey or game.

I never see any home cooking. All I
get is fancy stuff
Duke of Edinburgh

relishes &
pickles

Hot Pepper Relish

*6 firm cucumbers, peeled,
de-seeded and chopped*
*1 red and 1 green pepper,
de-seeded and chopped*
*450 g (1 lb) onions,
chopped*
*2 chillies de-seeded and
chopped*
30 g (1 oz) salt
300 ml (1 pint) water
*450 ml (¾ pint) cider
vinegar*
*300 g (10 oz) granulated
sugar*
1 teaspoon mustard seed
2 teaspoons celery seeds
½ teaspoon turmeric

*Quantity: approx 1.5 litres
(2½ pints)*
*Storage: vacuum-sealed,
1 year*

Put the cucumber, peppers, onions and chilli peppers in a bowl. Add the salt and water. Stir well before covering and leaving in a cool place overnight. The next day strain in a colander, set over a large bowl. Leave to drain for an hour, turning the vegetables over once or twice so that they drain well. Place the vinegar, sugar and spices in a non-aluminium saucepan. Add the drained vegetables and bring slowly to the boil. Boil for 10 minutes.

Then ladle into hot, sterilised jars, cover, and seal immediately with non-metallic lids or Cellophane.

THIS COMBINES SWEET and sour and heat most agreeably.

Corn Relish

340 g (12 oz) corn kernels,
cut from the cob
2 medium-size onions,
chopped
340 g (12 oz) fresh
tomatoes, peeled, de-
seeded and chopped
340 g (12 oz) cucumber,
peeled, de-seeded and
chopped
300 g (10 oz) cabbage,
chopped finely
340 g (12 oz) granulated
sugar
2 teaspoons salt
1 tablespoon celery or
fennel seeds
750 ml (1¼ pints) cider
vinegar

Quantity: 2.25 litres
(4 pints)
Storage: vacuum-sealed,
1 year

Place all the ingredients in a large non-aluminium saucepan. Bring to the boil, reduce the heat and simmer (uncovered) for about 20 minutes until thick.

Pour into hot, sterilised jars, cover, and seal at once with non-metallic lids or Cellophane.

Red Pepper Mustard

6 large red peppers
2 tablespoons dry mustard
2 tablespoons dark brown
    sugar
a dash of Tabasco sauce
125 ml (scant ¼ pint) cider
    vinegar
125 ml (scant ¼ pint)
    water
2 tablespoons sherry
1 tablespoon mustard seeds
a pinch of dried oregano

Quantity: 600 ml (1 pint)
Storage: refrigerated,
    4 months

Place the peppers (whole) under a hot grill until they are charred and blistered on all sides. Put them in a paper bag or bowl covered with cling film until they are cool enough to handle. Then peel off the skins and discard. Remove the seeds and core and discard. Finely chop one of the peppers and set it aside. Purée the remaining peppers in a blender or food processor. Mix the dry mustard, sugar, Tabasco, vinegar and water together in a small bowl. Cover and set aside. Place the pepper purée, sherry, mustard seeds and oregano in a non-aluminium saucepan and bring to a boil. Add the dry mustard mixture and simmer, stirring occasionally, until the mixture thickens. Stir in the reserved chopped pepper and pour into sterilised jars. Cover and seal at once with non-metallic lids or Cellophane.

A SPOONFUL OF this in a vinaigrette will give a lovely lift to salads and it is also incredibly good in roast beef sandwiches.

Calvados Fruit Relish
Red Pepper Mustard
Exotic Fruit Relish

Calvados Fruit Relish

*5 tomatoes, peeled, de-
    seeded and chopped*
*2 pears, peeled, cored and
    chopped*
*2 peaches, peeled, stoned
    and chopped*
*1 red pepper, de-seeded and
    chopped*
*1 medium-size onion,
    chopped finely*
*4 cm (1½-inch) piece of
    ginger, peeled and then
    grated*
*350 ml (12 fl oz) cider
    vinegar*
*340 g (12 oz) light-brown
    sugar*
1 teaspoon fennel seeds
*1 teaspoon ground
    cinnamon*
150 ml (¼ pint) Calvados

*Quantity: 900 ml
    (1½ pints)*
*Storage: vacuum-sealed,
    1 year*

Place all the ingredients, except the Calvados, in a non-aluminium preserving pan or saucepan. Bring to a boil, lower the heat and simmer (uncovered) for about 1 hour or until the relish has thickened. Stir occasionally to prevent the mixture sticking. Remove from the heat, stir in the Calvados, and pour into warm, sterilised jars. Cover and seal immediately with non-metallic lids or Cellophane. Keep for 4 weeks before using.

Exotic Fruit Relish

1 tomato, chopped

1 mango, chopped

140 g (5 oz) fresh
   pineapple, peeled and
   chopped

2 kiwi-fruit, peeled and
   chopped

1 eating apple, peeled,
   cored and chopped

85 g (3 oz) white seedless
   grapes

4 shallots, peeled and sliced

2.5 cm (1-inch) piece of
   fresh ginger, peeled and
   chopped finely

5 cloves

a stick of cinnamon

6 allspice berries

1–2 dried chilli peppers

½ teaspoon fennel seeds

170 g (6 oz) demerara
   sugar

175 ml (6 fl oz) cider
   vinegar

60 g (2 oz) pine kernels

2 tablespoons fruit liqueur,
   such as Grand Marnier

Quantity: 600 ml (1 pint)
Storage: vacuum-sealed,
   1 year

Place all but the last 2 ingredients in a non-aluminium saucepan. Bring to a boil and boil uncovered for about 25 minutes until the mixture is thick. The fruit should still retain its shape. Stir in the pine kernels and ladle into 2 sterilised jars. Pour a tablespoon of the liqueur over the top of each jar. Then cover and seal with non-metallic lids or Cellophane. Store in a cool, dry and dark place and leave for 6 weeks before using.

THE FRUITS FOR this relish can be varied. Choose a mixture of acid and sweet fruits to keep a similar balance. Pecans or walnuts can replace the pine kernels.

Spiced Asian Pears

450 ml (¾ pint) mild red
   wine vinegar
150 ml (¼ pint) dry red
   wine
680 g (1½ lb) granulated
   sugar
5 cm (2-inch) piece of fresh
   ginger, peeled and sliced
5 cm (2-inch) stick of
   cinnamon
10 allspice berries
4 blades of mace
8 cloves
925 g (2 lb) Asian pears

Quantity: 900 ml
   (1½ pints)
Storage: vacuum-sealed,
   6 months
   refrigerated, 4 months

Combine all the ingredients, except the pears, in a large non-aluminium saucepan and bring slowly to the boil. Peel, quarter, core and slice the pears and place them in a large bowl. Pour the hot liquid over them, cover, and leave overnight. The next day pour all the contents of the bowl into the saucepan and simmer for 15 minutes. Remove the pears with a slotted spoon and pack into sterilised, hot preserving jars. Re-boil the syrup, pour over the pears and seal the jars at once with non-metallic lids or Cellophane. Keep for at least 4 weeks before using.

UNLIKE ORDINARY PEARS, Asian pears remain hard when they are ripe so it is important to select those that are the most aromatic. They are perfect for spicing, because they retain their crisp texture and refreshing flavour even after being poached.

Pickled limes;

Spiced Asian Pears

Pickled Lemons or Limes

Scrub the lemons or limes with hot water and soap and rinse very well. Then cut the fruit into slices. Sprinkle lavishly with salt and leave in a colander to soften for at least 24 hours. Do not rinse off the salt. Arrange the slices in layers in a glass jar, sprinkling each layer with paprika. Cover the slices completely with a light olive oil. Cover with a tight-fitting lid and store in a cool dry place. They will be ready to eat in about 3 weeks.

A RECIPE OF Claudia Roden's. Pickled lemons and limes are used in many Moroccan casseroles and salads and you will find them useful for many other dishes. A few slices of either the lemon or lime, with a bit of the oil they are packed in, are good cooked with baked fish. In an air-tight jar they will keep for 6 months or more.

Pickled Prunes

925 g (2 lb) dried prunes
1 China-tea bag
water
450 g (1 lb) sugar
450 ml (¾ pint) cider
  vinegar
6 cloves
3 tablespoons allspice
  berries
a stick of cinnamon
a 2.5 cm (1-inch) piece of
  fresh ginger, peeled
zest of 1 lemon, cut into
  strips

Quantity: 1.2 litres (2 pints)
Storage: vacuum-sealed,
  1 year

Place the prunes and tea bag in a bowl. Cover with boiling water and leave overnight. Using a large non-aluminium saucepan, dissolve the sugar in the vinegar over a gentle heat. Add the spices, lemon rind and prunes together with their soaking liquid. Boil very gently for 15 minutes. Remove the prunes and pack into hot, sterilised jars. Boil down the syrup for about 15 minutes until thick. Pour the syrup, including the spices, over the prunes to fill the jars before covering and sealing at once with non-metallic lids or Cellophane.

THESE MILDLY SPICED prunes go well with cold and hot meats, particularly pork. They can also be used in stuffings for, say, a boned shoulder of lamb.

Coriander Orange Slices

1.8 kg (4 lb) thin-skinned
  navel oranges
water
900 ml (1½ pints) cider
  vinegar
1.2 kg (2½ lb) sugar
2 sticks of cinnamon
2 teaspoons allspice berries
4 teaspoons coriander seeds,
  crushed slightly
12 cloves
6 cardamom pods, crushed
  slightly
6 blades of mace

Quantity: 1.2 litres
  (2 pints)
Storage: vacuum-sealed,
  1 year

Cut the oranges into 5 mm (¼-inch) slices. Place them in a large non-aluminium pan and just cover with water. Simmer, covered, for about 40 minutes until the peel is tender. Meanwhile, bring the vinegar, sugar and spices to the boil in another pan, and simmer for 5 minutes. Drain the cooked orange slices and reserve the cooking liquid. Place the drained fruit in the sugar syrup and, if necessary, add just enough reserved liquid to cover the fruit. Simmer, covered, for 35 minutes. Remove the pan from the heat and leave uncovered for 24 hours, turning the fruit in the syrup once or twice. The next day bring the fruit and syrup back to the boil. Drain the fruit and pack in jars. Arrange some slices to lie flat against the sides of the jars. Bring the syrup back to the boil and boil hard to thicken slightly. Pour over the slices, distributing the spices between the jars.

Cover and seal immediately with non-metallic lids or Cellophane. Store for at least 6 weeks before using.

SERVE A RING of these spicy orange slices around platters of cold meat.

Bread and Butter Pickles

925 g (2 lb) cucumbers
340 g (12 oz) onions, sliced
60 g (2 oz) salt
350 ml (12 fl oz) cider
  vinegar
340 g (12 oz) sugar
2 tablespoons mustard
  seeds
2 teaspoons celery seeds
¼ teaspoon turmeric
¼ teaspoon Cayenne
  pepper

Quantity: 1.2 litres (2 pints)
Storage: vacuum-sealed,
  6 months

Wash the cucumbers and then cut them (unpeeled) into 5 mm (¼-inch) slices. Place them with the onions and salt in a large bowl. Mix together well and leave for 3 hours. Drain the cucumber and onion, rinse under cold water and drain again. Bring all the other ingredients to the boil in a large non-aluminium pan. Then add the cucumbers and onions. Reduce the heat and simmer for 2 minutes. Do not allow it to boil or the finished pickles will be too limp.

Spoon the cucumbers and onions into warm, sterilised jars, cover with the liquid and spices and seal at once with non-metallic lids or Cellophane. Store for 2 weeks before using.

Papaya Pickle

225 g (8 oz) sugar
150 ml (¼ pint) cider
  vinegar
150 ml (¼ pint) water
1 small bay leaf
1 small stick of cinnamon
2 blades of mace
3 cloves
2 under-ripe papayas

Quantity: approx 900 ml
  (1½ pints)
Storage: vacuum-sealed,
  1 year

Bring all the ingredients, except the papaya, to the boil in a non-aluminium pan, and simmer for a few minutes. Meanwhile, peel, halve and de-seed the papayas. Cut each half into small chunks and add these to the syrup. Simmer gently for 15 minutes. Then cover and seal at once with non-metallic lids or Cellophane. Leave for several weeks before using.

PARTICULARLY GOOD WITH game and poultry.

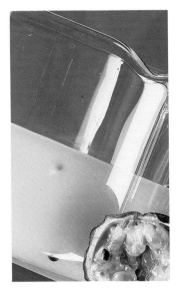

Cuisine is when things taste like
themselves
Curnonsky

syrups & sauces

White Chocolate Sauce

70 g (2½ oz) unsalted
   butter, cut into small
   pieces
300 g (10 oz) white
   chocolate, cut into small
   pieces
150 ml (¼ pint) double
   cream
1 tablespoon Kirsch or other
   fruit liqueur

Quantity: 600 ml (1 pint)
Storage: refrigerated,
   2 weeks
   frozen, 6 months

Place the butter, chocolate and cream in the top of a double saucepan set over barely simmering water and stir until smooth. Add the liqueur, and pour into a container. Cover and refrigerate or freeze. Re-heat in a double saucepan before serving.

SERVE THIS WITH a good dark chocolate ice cream or a slice of chocolate cake or mousse.

Caramel Brandy Pecan Sauce

260 g (9 oz) caster sugar
50 ml (2 fl oz) cold water
150 ml (¼ pint) hot water
2 tablespoons brandy
45 g (1½ oz) shelled
   pecans, chopped

Quantity: 300 ml (½ pint)
Storage: refrigerated,
   6 weeks

Place the sugar and cold water in a small heavy-bottomed saucepan. Bring to the boil without stirring. Then boil, swirling the pan occasionally so that it cooks evenly, until the mixture turns a good rich caramel colour. Remove from the heat and add the hot water. (Turn your face away as the caramel may spit.) Return the pan to the heat and stir until the caramel has dissolved. Remove from the heat and add the brandy. Pour into a container. Cool, then cover and refrigerate. Add the nuts before using.

Orange Whisky Sauce

170 g (6 oz) sugar
¼ teaspoon salt
2 tablespoons cornflour
grated zest of 1 orange and
    1 lemon
300 ml (½ pint) fresh
    orange juice
juice of 1 lemon
150 ml (¼ pint) boiling
    water
1 tablespoon butter
4 tablespoons whisky

Quantity: 450 ml (¾ pint)
Storage: refrigerated,
    2 weeks
    frozen, 6 months

Mix the sugar, salt, cornflour and zest in a saucepan. Stir in the orange juice, lemon juice and boiling water. Boil for 1 minute. Then remove from the heat and stir in the butter and whisky. Pour into jars and cover immediately. Refrigerate or freeze.

GOOD WITH CRÊPES and fruit salads or fresh strawberries.

Hot Fudge Sauce

60 g (2 oz) unsalted butter
6 tablespoons cocoa powder
    (not drinking chocolate)
5 tablespoons water
170 g (6 oz) sugar
2 tablespoons golden syrup
1 teaspoon vanilla essence

Quantity: 250 ml (8 fl oz)
Storage: refrigerated,
    4 weeks
    frozen, 6 months

Gently melt the butter with the cocoa over low heat. Add the water, sugar and syrup, bring to a simmer and boil together for 3 minutes. Pour into a glass jar and seal at once before refrigerating. Re-heat very gently before serving. Then stir in the vanilla.

HOT FUDGE SAUCE poured over vanilla ice cream is an unbeatable combination. Try sprinkling a few salted almonds over the top for an American-style sundae.

Raspberry and Redcurrant Sauce

140 g (5 oz) granulated
  sugar
150 ml (¼ pint) water
1 tablespoon liquid glucose
225 g (8 oz) redcurrants
450 g (1 lb) raspberries
juice of 1 lemon

Quantity: approx 900 ml
  (1½ pints)
Storage: refrigerated,
  1 week
  frozen, 3 months

Carefully dissolve the sugar in the water and glucose over a low heat. Bring to the boil, stirring occasionally with a wooden spatula. Boil for 2 minutes. Remove from the heat and cool. Remove the stalks from the redcurrants and place them in a blender or food processor with the raspberries, sugar syrup and lemon juice. Blend until smooth and then rub through a strainer. Refrigerate, (covered) if using within 5 days; otherwise freeze.
Note: Other fruit sauces can be made in the same way. Use 680 g (1½ lb) of one kind of soft fruit (such as apricots or strawberries).

Kahlúa Sauce

120 g (4 oz) good dark
  chocolate
140 g (5 oz) unsalted butter
30 g (1 oz) cocoa powder
2 tablespoons instant
  espresso coffee powder
140 g (5 oz) light brown
  sugar
6 tablespoons single cream
6 tablespoons Kahlúa or
  other coffee liqueur

Quantity: 600 ml (1 pint)
Storage: refrigerated,
  1 month
  frozen, 6 months

Melt the chocolate and butter together in the top of a double saucepan set over simmering water. Stir in the cocoa, the instant coffee and sugar, and then add the cream and coffee liqueur. Cook until the syrup thickens slightly. Then pour into sterilised jars and cover at once. Refrigerate or freeze when cool.

SERVE WARM OVER ice cream, cake or vanilla pudding.

Mango Passion-fruit Sauce;
Kahlúa Sauce;
Spiced Blueberry Syrup;
Raspberry and Redcurrant Sauce

Spiced Blueberry Syrup

680 g (1½ lb) fresh
   blueberries
juice of 2 lemons
juice of 1 orange
½ teaspoon ground
   cinnamon
a small pinch of ground
   cloves
several gratings of fresh
   nutmeg
200 g (7 oz) granulated
   sugar
1 tablespoon cornflour
a little cold water
120 g (4 oz) unsalted
   butter, cut into small
   pieces
a pinch of salt

Quantity: 900 ml
   (1½ pints)
Storage: refrigerated,
   1 month

Place the blueberries, lemon and orange juice,
spices and sugar in a heavy-bottomed
saucepan and bring to the boil. Lower the
heat and simmer gently for 15 minutes.
Dissolve the cornflour in 3 tablespoons of
cold water and then add to the blueberries.
Simmer for another few minutes. Then
remove from the heat and stir in the butter, a
few bits at a time. When the butter is blended
into the sauce, pour into jars and cover at
once. Refrigerate when cool.

Mango Passion-fruit Sauce

2 ripe mangoes
juice of 1 orange
juice of 1 lime
2 passion-fruit
icing sugar

Quantity: approx 600 ml
   (1 pint)
Storage: refrigerated,
   2 weeks

Peel the mangoes and chop the flesh. Purée in a blender with the orange juice. Turn into a bowl and stir in the lime juice. Cut each passion-fruit in half, scoop out the insides with a small spoon, and work the juice through a strainer into the bowl. Sift a few tablespoons of icing sugar on top of the purée and stir to blend. Taste for flavour – you are after a sharp, yet sweet, taste. Add more sieved icing sugar or lime juice as necessary. Cover the bowl and refrigerate.

THIS IS LOVELY on fruit salads.

Rum Raisin Syrup

170 g (6 oz) caster sugar
120 g (4 oz) dark-brown
   soft sugar
600 ml (1 pint) water
1 tablespoon liquid glucose
   (optional)
grated zest of 1 lime
250 ml (8 fl oz) dark rum
60 g (2 oz) seedless raisins
60 g (2 oz) shelled pecans
   or walnuts, chopped
   (optional)

Quantity: 600 ml (1 pint)
Storage: vacuum-sealed,
   1 year

Place the sugars, water, and glucose in a heavy-bottomed saucepan. Bring to the boil over a medium heat, without stirring, until the sugar has dissolved. Simmer for 15 minutes, or until the syrup is quite thick. Remove the pan from the heat and stir in the zest of lime and the rum. If you are planning to vacuum-seal, bring the syrup back to a boil before bottling. Otherwise store in sealed jars in the refrigerator.

Pomegranate Syrup

2 large ripe pomegranates
juice of 1 lemon
granulated sugar

Quantity: 450 ml (¾ pint)
Storage: refrigerated,
  4 weeks
  frozen, 6 months

Score the skin of the pomegranates into quarters without piercing the flesh. Break the fruit in half and in half again, following the score lines. Bend back the rind and pull out the seeds. Discard the yellowish membrane, weigh the seeds and place them with an equal amount of sugar and the lemon juice in a bowl. Cover and leave overnight in a cool place. Place the mixture in a stainless-steel saucepan and bring to the boil. Lower the heat and simmer for 2 minutes. Strain, pressing through as much of the juice as possible. Pour into sterilised jars and refrigerate when cool.

Pomegranate Syrup;
Cranberry Rum Sauce;
Elderflower Syrup

Cranberry Rum Sauce

225 g (8 oz) granulated
  sugar
150 ml (¼ pint) water
a stick of cinnamon
3 cloves
a blace of mace
450 g (1 lb) cranberries
125 ml (4 fl oz) rum
2 teaspoons cornstarch

Quantity: 600 ml (1 pint)
Storage: vacuum-sealed,
  6 months

Place the sugar, water, cinnamon stick, cloves and mace in a saucepan and cook over a gentle heat until the sugar dissolves. Then boil over a medium-high heat for 10 minutes. Remove the spices and add the cranberries and all but 2 tablespoons of the rum. Cook for a further 10 minutes. Dissolve the cornstarch in the remaining rum and stir into the sauce. Simmer for another minute or two before pouring into hot jars and sealing at once.

USE OVER ICE cream, yogurt or puddings.

Elderflower Syrup

25 heads of elderflowers
1.6 kg (3½ lb) granulated
  sugar
1.75 litres (3 pints) boiled
  water, cold
60 g (2 oz) tartaric acid
2 lemons

Quantity: 1.75 litres
  (3 pints)
Storage: refrigerated, 3–4
  months
  frozen, 6 months

Shake the elderflower blossoms and place them in a large bowl with the sugar, water and tartaric acid. Scrub the lemons with soap and water and rinse them well. Then slice and add them to the bowl. Stir several times over a period of 24 hours. Then strain and bottle. Dilute to taste with soda water or mineral water.

THIS IS A great favourite of mine and is appreciated by everyone, children and adults alike, who drink it. It is well worth freezing some to have on hand during Lent as it makes an excellent non-alcoholic beverage for anyone who has given up alcohol. It is practically free if you have access to a park or live in the country.

Raspberry Caramel Sauce

170 g (6 oz) raspberries
170 g (6 oz) caster sugar
175 ml (6 fl oz) water
1 tablespoon lime juice
2 teaspoons eau de vie de
*   framboise*

Quantity: 300 ml (½ pint)
Storage: refrigerated,
*   4 weeks*
*   frozen, 6 months*

Place the raspberries in a food processor and purée. Strain through a fine sieve and set aside. Place the sugar, with half the water, in a small heavy-bottomed saucepan. Bring to the boil and cook until the sugar has turned a light caramel colour. Swirl the pan from time to time so that the sugar cooks evenly. Remove from the heat; add the rest of the water, turning your face away as the sugar spits. Return the pan to the heat and stir until the caramel is dissolved. Remove from the heat and stir in the raspberry purée and lime juice. Add the liqueur, pour into a sterilised jar and cover at once.

Spicy Apple Syrup

1.2 litres (2 pints) apple
*   juice made from whole*
*   apples (not a concentrate)*
2 sticks of cinnamon
4 cloves
6 blades of mace
2.5 cm (1-inch) piece of
*   fresh ginger, peeled and*
*   chopped*
3 thin strips of orange zest
30 g (1 oz) granulated
*   sugar (optional)*
3 tablespoons Calvados

Quantity: 600 ml (1 pint)
Storage: refrigerated,
*   4 weeks*
*   frozen, 6 months*

Place all the ingredients, except the sugar and Calvados, in a heavy-bottomed, non-aluminium saucepan. Cook over a medium heat until the apple juice comes to the boil. Then lower the heat and simmer for 15 minutes. Remove from the heat, cover, and leave for 8 hours. Strain the syrup into a clean saucepan and simmer until it has reduced to a light syrup consistency. Add the Calvados, taste, and add the sugar if the syrup is too sour for your liking. Pour into hot, sterilised jars and seal at once. Cool before refrigerating.

C h e s t n u t s   i n   S y r u p

450 g (1 lb) chestnuts,
*   peeled weight*
225 g (8 oz) granulated
*   sugar*
225 g (8 oz) powdered
*   glucose (available at*
*   chemists)*
175 ml (6 fl oz) water
1 teaspoon vanilla essence

Quantity: 1.2 litres (2 pints)
Storage: vacuum-sealed,
*   6 months*

Peel the chestnuts by cutting a cross through
the skin on their flat sides. Drop a few at a
time into a pan of boiling water. Leave for
4 minutes or so and then remove with a
slotted spoon. Peel off both the inner and
outer skins. Wear rubber gloves so that you
can handle the hot chestnuts without burning
your fingers. (Alternatively the nicked
chestnuts can be set on a dish and placed in a
microwave oven for about 3 minutes, on high,
then peeled). Put the sugar, glucose and
water in a pan large enough to hold the
chestnuts and heat gently until the sugars are
dissolved. Then bring to the boil. Take the pan
off the heat, add the chestnuts, return to the
heat and bring back to the boil. Remove from
the heat, cover the pan, and leave overnight at
room temperature. The next day bring the pan
back to the boil and boil for 3 minutes,
uncovered. Remove from the heat, cover, and
leave again overnight. On the third day repeat
the boiling process. Remove from the heat,
stir in the vanilla and pour both syrup and
chestnuts into hot sterilised jars. Seal at once
and label.

THESE ARE NOT quite the same as marrons
glacés but are just as delicious, and can be
used as a sauce for ice cream or eaten as a
dessert with brandy-flavoured whipped
cream.

The fruit clothes itself with flavour

Andre Gide

f r u i t s
in
a l c o h o l

Prunes in Wine

450 g (1 lb) prunes
1 China-tea bag
water
about 48 walnut halves
600 ml (1 pint) red wine
60 g (2 oz) sugar
5 cm (2-inch) piece of
  cinnamon stick
4 cloves

Quantity: 1.25 litres
  (2¼ pints)
Storage: refrigerated,
  5 weeks

Place the prunes and tea bag in a bowl. Cover them in boiling water and leave overnight to soften. The next day stone the prunes and stuff each with a walnut half. Pack into sterilised jars. Bring the wine, sugar, cinnamon stick and cloves to a boil, and simmer for 5 minutes. Remove from the heat, cover, and leave to cool. Fill the jars with the strained wine and seal. Store in the refrigerator. Leave for 5 days before using and serve at room temperature.

A TREAT TO have tucked away in the refrigerator.

Romtopf

This is a glorious way of preserving fruit for Christmas and it couldn't be easier. All you need is a large glass jar with a tight-fitting lid, a variety of soft summer fruit, some rum and granulated or caster sugar. Start with the first strawberries and make a layer of them in the bottom of the jar. Sprinkle with sugar and cover with either eau de vie, rum or brandy. Add more fruit as it comes into season, sprinkling each layer with sugar and covering with the spirit you are using. Peaches, nectarines, and cherries should be skinned and stoned before being used. Choose contrasting colours of fruit for the layers. Avoid rhubarb, apples and melon. Store the jar in a cool, dark place and leave for at least 3 months before using. Serve spoonfuls over ice cream or in small glasses with a dollop of whipped cream. You can also fill small jars with the romtopf to offer as presents. It will keep for a year or more.

Clementines in Armagnac

*300 g (10 oz) granulated
  sugar*
*6 green cardamom pods,
  crushed*
600 ml (1 pint) water
450 g (1 lb) clementines
Armagnac

Quantity: 600 ml (1 pint)
*Storage: refrigerated,
  6 months*

Place the sugar, cardamom pods and water in a saucepan. Bring to the boil carefully to dissolve the sugar and then boil for 5 minutes. Wash the fruit and remove any stalks or flower ends. Make 4 or 5 pricks in each clementine with a darning needle so that the fruit will absorb the syrup. Add the fruit to the syrup and simmer gently for about 1 hour, or until the skins are soft. Carefully spoon the fruit from the pan into a sterilised 600 ml (1 pint) glass jar. Pour in enough Armagnac to come half-way up the fruit. Add enough syrup to cover the fruit. Then seal at once and carefully reverse the jar to blend the liquids. Store in a cool dark place for at least 2 weeks before using.

SERVE THESE CLEMENTINES thinly sliced with puddings, ice cream and cakes; or enjoy them on their own with a dollop of mascarpone cream cheese or clotted cream.

Peaches in Brandy

680 g (1½ lb) peaches,
  white-fleshed if possible
340 g (12 oz) granulated
  sugar
450 ml (¾ pint) water
5 cm (2-inch) piece of
  cinnamon stick
5 cloves
6–8 tablespoons brandy

Quantity: 600 ml (1 pint)
Storage: refrigerated,
  4 weeks

Drop the peaches, one at a time, into simmering water and leave them for around 10 seconds. Remove the peaches with a slotted spoon. Then peel off the skin, cut in half and remove the stones. Combine the sugar and water in a non-aluminium saucepan and bring to the boil. Add the spices and boil for 4 minutes, then add the peach halves and simmer for another 4 minutes, or until the peaches are lightly poached. Carefully place the peaches in glass jars using a slotted spoon. Distribute the brandy between the jars and top up with the strained syrup. Seal at once. Cool and then store in the refrigerator. Leave for one week before eating.

Pineapple in Kirsch

1 large pineapple
170 g (6 oz) granulated
   sugar
600 ml (1 pint) water
8 tablespoons Kirsch

Quantity: 1 litre (1¾ pints)
Storage: refrigerated,
   3 weeks

Cut off the top and bottom of the pineapple and remove the skin. Cut the flesh into 1 cm (½-inch) slices. Remove the centre core and discard. Cut the rings into 6 equal-size wedges. Bring the sugar and water carefully to the boil in a large non-aluminium saucepan. Add the pineapple and poach for 4 minutes. Strain the pineapple reserving the syrup. Place the pineapple in sterilised jars, divide the Kirsch between the jars, and add enough syrup to cover. Seal immediately. Refrigerate when cool.

A m a r e t t o   A p r i c o t s

*450 g (1 lb) whole dried
    apricots*
*85 g (3 oz) granulated
    sugar*
juice of 1 orange
1 litre (1¾ pints) water
*60 g (2 oz) whole blanched
    almonds*
*150 ml (¼ pint) Amaretto
    liqueur*

Quantity: 600 ml (1 pint)
*Storage: refrigerated,
    6 months*

Place the apricots, sugar, orange juice and
water in a saucepan. Bring slowly to the boil,
reduce the heat and simmer gently for
15 minutes, or until the apricots are tender.
Strain the apricots, return the syrup to the
saucepan and boil for 15 minutes to thicken
the syrup. Place the apricots and almonds in
sterilised warm jars. Divide the Amaretto
liqueur between the jars, then fill almost to
the top with the reserved syrup. Seal the jars
at once. Store in the fridge for 3 weeks before
serving.

APRICOT FOOLS AND mousses made with
these apricots are extra special. They are also
delicious stirred in yogurt or added to fruit
salads.

Figs in Cognac

*120 g (4 oz) vanilla sugar or
    caster sugar
175 ml (6 fl oz) water
12 figs
175 ml (6 fl oz) Cognac*

*Quantity: approx 900 ml
    (1½ pints)
Storage: refrigerated,
    5 weeks*

Heap the sugar in the centre of a heavy saucepan. Pour the water around the edges and bring to the boil carefully to dissolve the sugar. Boil for 2 minutes then set aside to cool. Peel and quarter the figs and pack them into 2 or 3 sterilised jars. Divide the Cognac between the jars and top up with the sugar syrup. Seal at once and store in thé refrigerator. Shake the jars occasionally.

THESE MAKE A most delicious dessert served with crème fraîche.

Chestnuts in Kirsch

1 kg (2¼ lb) chestnuts
310 g (11 oz) granulated
*   sugar*
200 ml (8 fl oz) water
juice of 1 lemon
450 ml (¾ pint) Kirsch

Quantity: 1.5 litre
*   (2½ pints)*
Storage: refrigerated,
*   6 months*

Cut a cross through the skin on the flat side of each chestnut. Place a few nuts at a time in a pan of boiling water. Boil for 3–4 minutes. Then peel off both outer and inner skins. Wear rubber gloves so that you can work while the chestnuts are still very hot. Change the boiling water when it becomes too brown from the chestnuts. When all the chestnuts are peeled, place them in a clean pan of boiling water and simmer for about 8 minutes until tender. Drain the chestnuts and place in sterilised jars. Carefully heat the sugar, water and the lemon juice together until the sugar dissolves. Then bring to the boil. Remove from the heat and when the syrup is cool add the Kirsch. Pour over the chestnuts, covering them completely. Seal at once and store in the fridge.

C h e r r y   B r a n d y

450 g (1 lb) morello
  cherries, stoned weight
225 g (8 oz) caster sugar
600 ml (1 pint) brandy
a piece of cinnamon stick

Quantity: 1 litre (1¾ pints)
Storage: sealed, indefinite
  time

Prick the fruit with a darning needle and place them in a large jar. Add the caster sugar, brandy and cinnamon stick. Seal the jar and store in a dark place for 3 months, shaking the jar occasionally. Filter the brandy through a muslin-lined sieve and bottle. Seal with either tight-fitting lids or corks. Cherry brandy improves with age. The cherries are delicious served with vanilla ice cream.

Note: Bing or other varieties of eating cherries can be used in the same way but reduce the sugar slightly.

Cooking is like love. It should be
entered into with abandon or not at all
Harriet Van Horne

cordials
&
liqueurs

Curaçao

2 oranges
600 ml (1 pint) eau de vie
   or brandy
4 cm (1½-inch) piece of
   cinnamon stick
225 g (8 oz) caster sugar

Quantity: 600 ml (1 pint)
Storage: sealed, indefinite
   time

Scrub the oranges with soap and water, rinse them well and then dry them. Grate the zest from the oranges and place it in a jar. Add the alcohol and cinnamon stick, cover and leave for 1 week. Strain the liquor into a clean jar, add the sugar, and seal. Leave for at least 4 weeks before using, shaking occasionally until the sugar has dissolved. This liqueur improves with age.

Strawberry Liquor

225–260 g (8–9 oz)
  strawberries, hulled
225–260 g (8–9 oz) caster
  sugar
300 ml (½ pint) vodka or
  gin

Quantity: 300 ml (½ pint)
Storage: sealed, indefinite
  time

Fill a large bottling jar with the clean, but unwashed, strawberries. (Any water you use for washing the strawberries dilutes the taste, so if you have to wash them, dry them well using a tea-towel). Pour caster sugar one-third of the way up the jar and then fill to the brim with vodka or gin. Seal and leave in a cool dark place, turning over occasionally, for 2 months. When ready, strain the liquor through a muslin-lined sieve into bottles. Then seal using tight-fitting lids or corks, and label. Serve the strawberries with ice cream; or purée them and add to a sugar syrup to make a peppy sauce.

Crème de Cassis

1 kg (2¼ lb) blackcurrants
1 litre (1¾ pints)
  reasonably good red wine
1.3 kg (3 lb) granulated
  sugar
900 ml (1½ pints) brandy,
  gin or vodka

Quantity: 1.5 litres
  (2½ pints)
Storage: sealed, 1 year

Soak the blackcurrants and wine together in a bowl for 48 hours. Put a large piece of old sheeting into a large basin. Add the currants and wine, in batches, to a blender and purée. Turn the mush into the sheet-lined basin. Pull the cloth together and squeeze out all the liquid. Measure this liquid, put it into a preserving pan and for each litre (1¾ pints) add 1½ kg (2 lb) of sugar. Place over a low heat and stir until the sugar is dissolved. Regulate the heat so that the liquid keeps above blood temperature (37°C/98.4°F) but well below simmering and boiling points; use a thermometer to make sure. Check the temperature after 15 minutes and give the mixture a good stir. Do this several more times. In about 2 hours the syrup will have reduced slightly and look somewhat syrupy. Leave to cool. Add three parts of the blackcurrant syrup to one part brandy or other spirit. Pour through a funnel into bottles, put on either tight-fitting lids or corks, and label. Leave for at least 2 days before using.

THE RAGE FOR Kir and Kir Royale has made Crème de Cassis an everyday liqueur. Apart from its use with wine and champagne it can also be added to sauces and puddings. Just a few spoonfuls are all that are needed. This recipe is from Jane Grigson.

Vanilla Brandy;
Strawberry Liquor;
Maracudja;
Crème de Cassis

M a r a c u d j a

120 g (4 oz) light-brown
   sugar
6 tablespoons water
14 passion-fruit
400 ml (14 fl oz) light rum

Quantity: 900 ml
   (1½ pints)
Storage: sealed, 6 months

Heat the sugar and water in a small heavy-bottomed saucepan until the sugar dissolves, and then leave to cool. Cut the passion-fruit in half, scoop out the flesh and seeds and spoon these into a glass jar. Add the rum and sugar syrup. Seal the jar with a tight-fitting lid and leave for at least 6 weeks. Adjust the taste if necessary by adding more rum or sugar syrup – it should not be too sweet. Served chilled.

MARACUDJA IS THE name for passion-fruit in Guadaloupe and this incredibly good apéritif from that country bears its name. When choosing passion-fruit select those that are the least crinkled.

V a n i l l a   B r a n d y

2 vanilla pods
300 ml (½ pint) brandy

Quantity: 300 ml (½ pint)
Storage: sealed, indefinite
   time

Split the vanilla pods in half vertically and store them in a bottle of brandy. Shake it occasionally and leave for 3 months before using.

EVERY KITCHEN SHOULD have a bottle of this at hand. It is invaluable for flavouring Christmas puddings or cakes, fruit puddings or whipped cream.

Apricot Liqueur

580 g (1¼ lb) large ripe
*   apricots*
4 green cardamom pods,
*   crushed*
1 litre (1¾ pints) dry white
*   wine*
450 g (1 lb) granulated
*   sugar*
½ litre (scant pint) vodka

Quantity; 1.5 litres
*   (2½ pints)*
Storage: sealed, 6 months

Place the apricots, cardamom pods and wine in a non-aluminium saucepan and bring to the boil. Remove from the heat and stir in the sugar until it has dissolved. Then add the vodka. Cover with cling-film and leave for 4 days to infuse. Strain through a muslin-lined sieve. Then bottle the liqueur and seal either with tight-fitting lids or corks.

Elderflower Champagne

680 g (1½ lb) granulated
   sugar
4 litres (1 gallon) water
2 lemons
6 large heads of elderflowers
2 tablespoons white wine
   vinegar

Quantity: 4 litres (1 gallon)
Storage: sealed, 3 months

Place the sugar in a large bowl. Boil the water and pour it over the sugar, stirring until it is dissolved. Scrub the lemons with a mild soap and rinse well. Squeeze the lemons and add both the juice and quartered skins to the bowl. Add the elderflowers and vinegar, cover with a thick cloth, and leave for 24 hours. Squeeze the flowers to extract all the flavour, before discarding them. Then strain the liquid through a muslin-lined sieve. Store in large bottles and cork securely. This can be used from 14 days onwards.

EVERY HOUSEHOLD SHOULD have a gallon or two of this very inexpensive and deliciously refreshing drink in their wine cellar. Serve it chilled. Pick the flowers on a dry day and choose fragrant heads.

Woe to the cook whose sauce has no
sting
Chaucer

v i n e g a r s
o i l s

Garlic Oil

300 ml (½ pint) extra-
  virgin olive oil
1 tablespoon minced garlic

Quantity: 300 ml (½ pint)
Storage: sealed, 1 year

Combine the oil and garlic in a jar with a tight-fitting lid. Leave for 3–4 days at room temperature. Strain, discarding the garlic (or use it for another purpose). Bottle the oil and label.

IF YOU USE this oil for cooking you may want to add more minced garlic as you cook, because heating garlic oil mellows its flavour. For salads it can be combined with other oils for a more subtle dressing.

Spiced Vinegar

2.25 litres (4 pints) cider
  vinegar
85 g (3 oz) granulated
  sugar
2 tablespoons celery seed
2 tablespoons mustard seed
2 tablespoons black
  peppercorns, crushed
2 tablespoons green
  cardamom pods
1 tablespoon each of whole
  cloves, coriander seeds
  and allspice berries
a stick of cinnamon
5 cm (2-inch) piece of fresh
  ginger, sliced
4 garlic cloves, crushed
1 dried chilli
Quantity: 2.25 litres
  (4 pints)
Storage: sealed, 1 year

Combine all the ingredients in a large non-aluminium saucepan. Bring slowly to just below boiling point. Remove from the heat and pour into one or more glass jars. Leave in a dark place for 3–4 weeks before straining and bottling.

Herbed Olive Oil

4 sprigs fresh marjoram
2 sprigs fresh rosemary
2 small bay leaves
*450 ml (¾ pint) mild olive
    oil*

Quantity: 450 ml (¾ pint)
Storage: sealed, 6 months

Combine the herbs with the olive oil and keep in a well-closed bottle. Leave for at least 6 days at room temperature before using.

NOTHING COULD BE simpler than making a herbed oil and it will prove very useful for marinades or basting meat and poultry, as well as for salad dressings. Fresh herbs should be rinsed quickly and dried before being added to the oil. Dried herbs should be crushed in a mortar, then heated slightly in the oil to bring out the flavour.

Raspberry Vinegar

*1 litre (1¾ pints) mild
    white wine vinegar*
*925 g (2 lb) fresh
    raspberries*

Quantity: 1 litre (1¾ pints)
Storage: sealed, 1 year

Place the vinegar with half the raspberries in a bowl. Cover and leave for 24 hours. The next day strain off the liquor and repeat with the remaining raspberries. Leave again for 24 hours. Then strain into clean bottles, cork, and store in a cool dark larder or cupboard.

RASPBERRY VINEGAR HAS many uses which have been brought to our attention by nouvelle cuisine chefs. Salads are dressed with it, beetroot is laced with it, and in very small amounts it will enhance sauces for duck or game. A simple raspberry vinegar sauce goes well with calf's liver and is quick to make.

Elderflower Vinegar

30 heads of elderflower
  blossoms
2.25 litres (4 pints) cider
  vinegar

Quantity: 2.25 litres
  (4 pints)
Storage: sealed, 1 year

Shake the blossoms to remove any insects. Then pull the blossoms away from the stems, using a fork. Combine the blossoms and vinegar in one or more wide-necked glass jars and stir to blend. Cover and leave on a window-sill or in the airing cupboard for 2–3 weeks. Strain through a muslin-lined sieve and bottle.

PARTICULARLY GOOD FOR marinades and meat salads.

Tarragon or other Herb Vinegar

2.25 litres (4 pints) cider
  vinegar
a large bunch of tarragon or
  other herb

Quantity: 2.25 litres
  (4 pints)
Storage: sealed, 1 year

Place the tarragon in the vinegar in a glass jar and leave on a sunny window-sill or in the airing cupboard for 2–3 weeks, shaking every few days. When the vinegar is flavoured to your liking, strain and bottle with a fresh sprig of the herb for identification.

SALADS HAVE BECOME such an important part of our diet that flavoured vinegars are much in demand. A selection in the store cupboard can help to inspire the creative cook.

Herbed Olive Oil;
Herb Vinegar;
Elderflower Vinegar;
Spiced Vinegar

Index